ALEM HAILU G/KRISTOS

Ouroboros

SELECTED
POEMS

Acknowledgments

I am indebted to God who helped me to undauntedly fight.
For page layout Tigist Seifu.

Dedicated to:-

Those fighting against all odds, lovers of poems and

poets.

Contents

.

Preface

After so many cold shoulders as well as twists and turns in the rocky road of penning poems in a foreign language and winning a broad array of fans, now , it doesn't come as a surprise for me to see some of my poems turning issues of discussion and contention. Nor does observing many identify and relate with the themes of my poems prove strange for me.

Through over five international poetry blogs I actively participate in, I have succeeded in acquiring a global presence. Floods of positive feedback from all corners of the globe, making a confluence, have begun to consummate my penmanship in poetry in a language that is not my own, English— the international medium of communication. The feedback laud my diction, the wide-range of messages I encode my poems with,the figurative speech I bring into play, the somersaults I make in a foreign language and the unique style I try to develop as a fingerprint. Some also appreciate how I harness poems to tell yarns.

Such encouragement-packed feedback fuel my passion of crafting poems. Pats on the back of this nature lend inspiration to me to congratulate myself in finding a niche as a poet. Above all things,the over 160 poems I wrote have begun to serve me sources of entertainment and amusement.

At times when I take time to reread them, they transport me to the wonderland of poetry. On such occasions I live over the eye-opener experience of reading poems. Currently, I also participate in some poem anthologies worldwide. Some of the anthologies aim at harnessing poems to change the world for the better such as fighting terrorism, upholding environmental stewardship and promoting justice, among others. This,in turn, has widened the scope of my recognition as a poet.

This book contains almost all of my poems, new ones and reviewed ones as well. I always try to side the truth, applaud achivements, comment on short falls and be forward looking. I belong to no political party or group. Some of my poems like ouroboros focus on African politics. Apart from entertaining, encouraging and enlightening, I use poems to convey social messages. I developed the skill of passing along social messages via reading literary pieces and translating the works of Maxim Gorky.

I use poetry to capture images and put pointed observations in light verse. It also helps me remain emotionally connected.

I hope you will enjoy this work of mine. I appreciate any feedback.

alemhailu2007@gmail.com

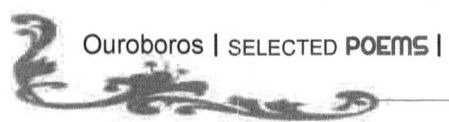

A 180-degree turn

The revolutionary ardent
Bordering on a prophet
For democracy's advent,
Up on grabbing
The rein of power,
With a superb
Acrobatic bent,
For a tyranny
An example set
For political thugs
To emulate!

A balm

The lapse of
An energetic lad
For the failure
Is news grand!
'Cause getting a balm
His scarred soul
Turns calm-
" I'm not single alone
With ill-fate-marked born!"

A bad habit

A hardcore addict
Than a habit resist
To the first allurement
You better put down
Your feet!

A bat

Early at night
If you see
A flying rat,
In a way
That is not right,
A zigzag,
Be sure it is a bat.

Sitting on
A big tree and
Winking with
A scornful eye
How the bat fly,
An owl
Mocks "It is foul!
It is foul!
It would be better
If bats crawl!"

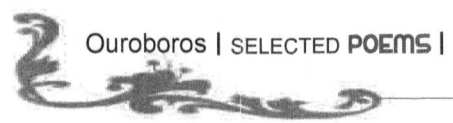
A better evil

A nationalist
He is incorrigible!

Carrot doesn't work
Let us try the stick, Off
power, him to kick!
Importing revolution,
Creating to dos
And escalating tension,
Galvanize we shall
Global attention
And also provoke
A flood of condemnation,
To the massacre
He commits
In a knee-jerk reaction!

Via our media outlets
Oft dishonest
To the truth and audience
Genocide we shall claim
His acts of self defense!

What is more under
Unfair sanction
Pressurize him we shall
To swelter and suffer
To suffer and swelter!

"This tyrant is not
A democrat
His throat
Ought be cut!
The mob,the people
Must know
We are a better evil
Though a mirror
Image of the devil!"

A black empress's legacy

I. Taytu Betul as a leader

Ethiopia is famed for being
A peaceful,hospitable
And warrior nation.
How come then it failed
To come to your attention,
As bees whose hive is threatened,
Citizens are ever alert
To foil provoked aggression!

The 1889 treacherous
Wuchale treaty
I will tear apart,
A messenger,with a tail
Between your legs,
Before you depart.

The Italian version
That tries to put Ethiopia,
A sovereign state,a pawn
Under Italy's protectorate
Is completely opposed to
What Ethiopia's
Versions indicate.
Till we meet
Your colonizing troops
At a showdown,
As a punitive measure to
A cheater or a clown
I will be tempted to smack
Your face
To ram home,valorous,
For fear we have no place.

II Taytu Betul a strategist

To deny the invading
Italian troops,advancing
From Eriteria,
Advantages of logistic,

We could do
The following trick
Indeed, we could shift
The battlefield
From Adigrat to Adwa
Also we could cut them
From a key water point
Till for truce they plead.
To this end,
A battalion
I will personally lead.
What is more,
I will inspire
Women, combatants,too
To fire!
Parallel to that
To nurse back
Our injured soldiers
Wounded in the attack
Also dry foods
To prepare and pack.

III Taytu Betul as a wife

Though independent,
With lots of love to
Emperor Menelik II,
My king and beloved husband,
I will lend a cooperative hand.

IV. A beacon of independence & standard bearer

True to my name Taytu
— A sunshine—
I will flicker
A ray of light
The oppressed for
Freedom to fight!

Women
For a military prowess,
Leadership and intelligence
Have acumen!

A broken heart suffice

When a
Remorseful convert,
Astray that had gone far
Blemishing his/her soul
With sin's tar,
Puts a broken heart
On the altar,
By far,
S/he could enjoy
God's grace
Or even
Win a higher place
In His face
Than a devotee,
Feeling proud
In his/her deed,
Speaks out loud
His/her spiritual war
Devil's way to bar.
It is with

A broken heart
The culprit
Hanged by the right
Of Jesus Christ
Got to Eden First
Though Adam,Moses,
Abraham,Job
And others were
Top on the shortlist.

It is by the virtue of
Their determination
Sinful ways to quit
Zacchaeus and
Mary Magdalene
Were seen fit
Than the hypocrite!
It is this line
From genesis
To revelation
God labours to bring
To our attention!
So with conviction

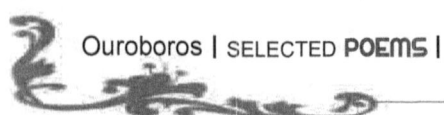
Let us pray for
Our soul's resurrection.
Of course no doubt
Our devotion could buttress
Our chance to enjoy
His mercilessness!

A corner

It is good giving emphasis
To concrete jungles
And infrastructural development,
But first leaders must learn to cut
A corner in their subjects' heart!

A far cry from

On Christmas,
When we mark
The savior's birth,
Taking the night out
For a nonstop bout
Running amok
Round the clock
Is a far cry
From Christendom!

Christ is not risen
For the season.
Oblivious to
" Give one
if you have two"
Hoarding twenty
Pairs of shoes
Under a lock
While others walk
Even without a sock
In Christendom

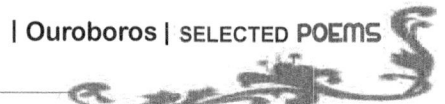
Doesn't work!

Don't you think
We have to visit the
Imprisoned and sick?
Also be polite
And considerate
With others
When we speak!

Humble,
Christ was born in a barn
So that display modesty
We can!

Christmas conveys
A message
Past description
About God's incarnation,
In the miracle
Saint Mary deserves
No less attention!

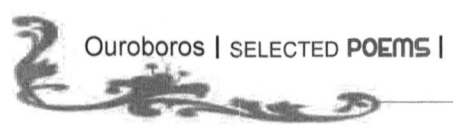

A genuine friend

S/he who
Our amity loves to cherish,

S/he who
The fulfillment of my wish
Has a bent to relish,

S/he who
Serves me a right arm
To parry,towards me,
Inflicted harm,

S/he who
Like a mirror
When I err
Gently draws my attention
To self-image
Tarnishing error,

S/he who
Basks in my success
Than covertly prove
An enemy adverse,

S/he who
Like a wolf
In a sheep skin
With my closest ones
Doesn't commit a sin—
Which to forget
But not to forgive
I will find hard
Before I am sent to
The graveyard,

S/he who
Like a cat or snake
A retaliatory measure
As a knee-jerk action
That does not take,
Also with
Gentle admonishment

Willing to forgive
My mistake,

S/he who
Without ifs and but,but...
My inborn follies
Willing to accept,

S/he who
During all seasons,
Agreeable or adverse,
A chameleon
His/her stance
That doesn't reverse,

S/he who
That doesn't
Behind my back gloat
When I lose
A battle fought,

When the aforementioned
Conditions set

Are met,
As gold is tested
With fire
A genuine friend
I will admire!

A genius taken for a dummy!

In musical notes composing
Ethiopia's giant
Saint Yared , irate, once
Opted to run away
From an ecclesiastical school
Dubbed by his priest teacher
An idiot and a fool
Worse still,
Looked down and ridiculed
By classmates, not cool.

Desirous to burn his boat
He trekked past a forest
And a pool
Determined never
To see those
Who cherish to pull

Over his eyes the wool.
Tired,he took a rest
By a tree shade
"I am good for nothing!"
Resonating in his head.

He continued
To lament his fate
Unaware God
Has a plan
To make him great.

While battling
To forget his pain
He saw a God-sent worm
Trying to climb a tree
Again,again,again,again
Again and again in vain!

To his surprise
The undaunted worm
Didn't fight shy,
In its seventh trial it

Managed to climb
The tree high
To enjoy the fruits laden
On the boughs
Outstretched to the sky!

Drawing a lesson
Saint Yared
Returned back to school
To outsmart all
Who took him for
A dummy and a fool!

At long last he
Pioneered in composing
Ten path-breaking
Musical notes that
Have no match
By any of, to date,
Succeeded batch!

Strange as it may appear,
Oblivious to

The unintentional
Piercing of his foot
By a king's spear,
Oblivious to his surrounding
Tuning his ear
To angels' orchestra to God,
Wholly engrossed, he was seen
With a similar passion,
Eye skyward, praising the Lord!

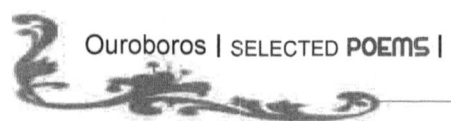

A hell turned paradise

My beloved
I always remember
Once, my soul
Had taken a ride
On a marital-bliss river
Jubilant nothing or no one
Could put us asunder.

But after I learnt
You have sown mistrust
On the fertile ground
Of my heart
When you cheated on me
Willfully letting
A cherished corner
To a lover another
The quiet donning
Ecstasy's river

Which I happily
Used to ride
Had taken leave
Forever
To uncharted water!

Bringing warmth
To my hearth,
Once you had made
My life a paradise on earth
Soon to change it to
An earthly hell
Worse than what sinners
Expect after death!

A herd mentality

If one pulls
A sheep astray
The flock is sure
To move that way.

To fish in a troubled water
De-constructing history
Thwart we could
The old social
Fabric of unity
And create we shall
A generation
Suffering a
Crisis of identity!

"Ask me not why
They are better than
My peers and I
Also sensitize me not
To deny,
What I see

With my naked eye!
In attire,
Grooving,life style,
Cosmetic application
And civilization
They galvanize
Youths'attention! "

Come up with
A generation
We shall
That does not bat
An eye
Our dictates to buy,
A generation
That does barter
A time-old culture
With fads, For such
a venture
Proves to it
An adventure.
Showing a
Seamstress acumen

We could promote an odd
Trouser that makes
A lad neither
A man nor a woman.

To achieve
What we
Terribly sought
If we use
Somebody of note,
Fame that has got
Say an artist or a poet,
The mob will not
Fight-shy to drink a lot
From our poison pot
Without a grain of salt
"God doesn't exist"
Could be top on the list!
Alas,we could say
"Worship us!
Or forget the Key-
And- Lock theory!
Why should you worry?"

Or social
And religious norms
We could rock
With "A lock could lock
A lock
Even in a wedlock!"

A kickback is not expected

There is nothing so stupid
As arguing with the stupid,
An eye for an eye,
Kickback an ass must I?

A king born

Once upon a time
There was an old king,
Who used to worry
About one thing
"Surely one day
I will pass away!"
As many me advise
Among my sons
The wise
An heir
Must take over
To govern
My subjects better.

Next to God,
To corporeal things
Who is above,
I want to check
The strength of
My sons' filial love.

Thus, his sons he called
To "How much
do you love me? " respond.
Answered the elder
"I love you like honey
That has no parallels any!"
He won the warm laughter
Of his father.
"I love you like sugar
Could honey be any better?"
Answered the second
Thus,a corner
He succeeded to cut
In his father's heart.

"I love you like a salt,
For there is no fault
As missing this ingredient
In any dish
We want to relish!"
Said the youngest
Proving the wisest.

"Come over here
Take over my throne
You are a king born!"
Replied the king
Feeling
From his heart
The lifting
Up of something!

A lake's obituary

The mob, elites, journalists
As well as poets like I
To our environment-unfriendly
Bent turning a blind eye
Also tardy in asking "Why we
Strip of mother nature's green mantle,
While to maintain the status quo
It gets locked in a sever battle?"
Equally not checking overgrazing,
We allowed fertile soil and sand
Amok,wild floods ride
To a close by touristic lake,
Whose mouth an expansion
Used to make
As much as its foreign body intake.

Soon,with the vast array of
Flora and fauna it supports,
Before we knew it
The magnificent lake died
Ceding place to a barren land,
An eyesore that looked a dump yard!

A linchpin that doesn't fit the axle

The hardest way
It came to my head,
If a linchpin doesn't fit
The axle,
It is as good as dead!

An honest man
Amid many a ragamuffin
Is just like one the last nail
Is hit on whose coffin!

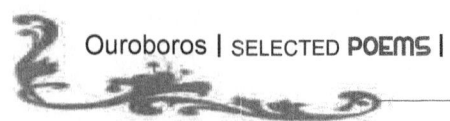

A martyr's eulogy

On my way to work,
Whenever I pass through
The Holy Trinity church,
After a brief prayer,
The tombstone of a martyr
My eyes never fail to search
As his eulogies sensitive cords
Are sure to touch!

I admire
The tombstone's design
A flickering torch,
Whose tongue
Is the martyr 's statue,
That talks loud his virtue!

"Holy Trinity
Till I crossed the river of death
Allegedly, striped of my health,
Poisoned by evil doers,
Who hanker

By unfair means
To amass wealth,
I had been
A public servant
Adherent to my faith! ''

"Holy Trinity
To abide by
Your commandment-
Don't steal-
Was my desire
Also to pull out millions
From poverty's quagmire.

Across-the-board development
Working better than one's best
Efficient resource utilization
Also drew my attention!''

"Holy Trinity
A generation
To corruption averse
Is all-out

The bad scenario
In my country
To reverse.
A generation for
A developmental thrust
That has lust.

I have come to understand
The coming up of
Many a lass and lad,
Whose rights that demand
I need no more reward,
When in front of you
This way I stand
Justice to demand! "

Children of Oromia,
Ethiopia's elephantine branch,
You have to detach
Your state, your country
From the impudent
And the corrupt
That still exercise

The outmoded
Colonizers'
Divide and rule
As a fool .

A corruption fighter
Development's workforce
Is also a hero
Like Ethiopia's
Valorous and dear sons
Balcha Abanefso
Geresu Duke,Abdisa Aga
And Jagama Kelo.

Children of Oromia
Giving to divisive guys
A deaf ear,
You should hold your
Country Ethiopia,
A cradle of mankind
And civilization, dear
Do not forget
Adding up

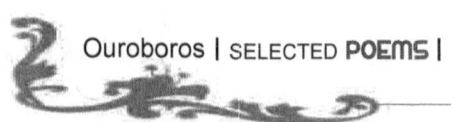
Is the current road map.

Evil doers
Killing a hero
Could not bring
The change drive
To zero.

As a poet what I can say
"Evil doers
Stop to opt for
Devilish way!
But if you
Keeping going astray
You will go
To the grave in
Ignominious way!"

A maverick seen

mentally sick

Parking his car
By the gate of a hospital
A man got into a bar,
From an eye-shot
Not far!

After a thief unfastened
The 4 bolts of a tyre,
The sale of which could
Help him make his day,
Seeing the owner
Approaching,
With the four bolts
He ran away.

Stranded, the owner
Was forced there to stay
At a loss what to do

And say!
"If you take a bolt
A tyre from the
Remaining three,
With three bolts each
All the tyres will agree
To allow the car move free!"
Advised him a man tall
Who, with patients'
Pajama, sat
On the hospital's wall
Observing all.

Doing so,
Thankful,the driver
Managed home to go!

On the morrow,
Taken by surprise
He wanted
That mentally sick
To speak.

Going to the hospital
"Tell me pal
With such intuition
How come
You join this hospital?"

"My friend,
If you deviate
From the normal
You are abnormal,
It is the likes of you,
The mentally sick,
That stranded me here
a maverick!"

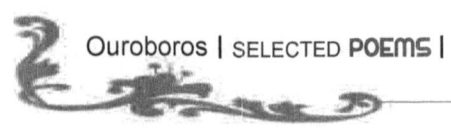
A painful satisfaction

Though monetary wise,
It doesn't promise to pay
I craft poems everyday,
For instance say

"Why my dream object,
To affections mine
Is adamant to reciprocate!"

The other way round,
Even if to acquaintances
Absurd,it may sound,
Some, I have to spend
My poems to newspapers
Magazines and
Websites to send!

For love of the labor,
I will never
Letup the endeavor!

There is a
Great deal of satisfaction

From sitting hours,
To put words into action,
Racking brain
And stretching imagination,
From the earth's core and crust
To the sky and firmament!

At night, when all is quiet,
Till I hit the nail
Right on the head,
I will not repair to bed!

Reading poems
Has satisfaction
No less, for it affords,
Handshakes,with poets
Of all ages,
Poets with poems
Of all color shades.

Probably the works
Of Shakespeare
That we hold dear!
What is more,Tagore.
In my duties
I will be remiss,

If I forget mention
Savo,Anna Akmatova,
Sara Teasdale
And Salomeja Neris.

Till getting a cherished corner
www.allpoery.com
www.writeoutloud.com
www.novelcollective.com
www.poemhunter.com
www.poetrypoems.com
www.hellopoetry.com
www.highonpoems.com
Ecstatic I was never!

Now,I peruse the websites
Of contemporary poets,
Displaying poetical prowess!

I want to add of course
An east African voice!

Out,a poem to digest
One could make a descent
Into wisdom's pit,

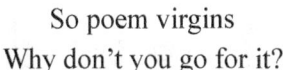
So poem virgins
Why don't you go for it?

From my experience,
For uplifting poems
'Start with Helen Steiner Rice!'
It is my advice.

A shifting goal post

Passionately playing dart
With cupid's arrow
To pierce your heart
I did squander
Many a year
Oblivious I am making
A blunder
Aiming at a goal post
That nonstop wander!

A shock treatment

When I regretted
Why God is stingy
In showering me
With wealth
He took my health
Goading me
With a threat of death!

Praying when
I recuperated
I realized
Foolishly I had been
Daydreaming for wealth
Oblivious my health
Is my number one wealth!

A slightest folly

A tiny crack or thick
Makes a ship sink
A slightest folly
Similarly could drain
A heart-full
Of love empty!

A stone can't

Of seniority
By default
You try to assume authority
But mind that
Though for a century
Under water comfortably sat,
Swim like a fish
A stone can't!

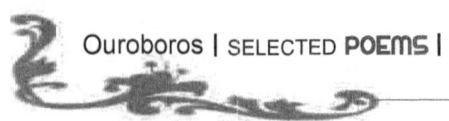

A sunflower

It is a mystery divine
With a radiant face
On par with a sunshine
You dictate and govern
The congealed
Sunflower soul of mine!

A sunny rain

Like walking
In a sunny rain
Yearning for you
In vain
Was a sugary pain!

A tight rope

All sides,
When darkness me envelop
Hopelessly, when unthinkable
Seems hope
A chimera, when the abyss
With saw-like teeth yawns
Expectant me to drop,
To cling on, to cross over
There is a tight rope,
God—for a single second
That doesn't stop
To emerge atop
Problems up that pop!

A tit for a tat

The pot called
The kettle "Black!"
The kettle rebuffed
" Pot, cry not foul,
Nor must you bark,
While it is stark,
You are a sooty reflection
Of a night, pitch-dark! "

While the blood of children,
The fair-sex,the feeble
And the old
Is still fresh in their hand,
Perpetrators of genocide
Demand,the less democrats,
Cursed and shunned
From a diplomatic mission,
Must step aside
By humanitarian law
As they don't abide!

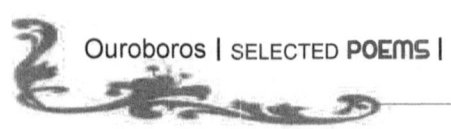

A toothless face

Slavishly touting laudatory
Remarks that
Run counter to his belief
Could not let a journalist
A moment's relief!

"The incumbent
Has flickered
Darkness-piercing light
Now as things are bright
Nonstop
We have to condemn the past
To catapult the present
On the infallible mast!"

Conveying messages
Without beef,
Also forced to turn
Eyes, to reality, deaf,
He is smote by
Excruciating grief
Freedom of expression

Turned brief!
To spare himself
A stomach pang
He has to allow
Political thugs,
In the guise of
Media bosses
That form
Government's favor
Ingratiating gang,
His mouth to gag!

Intimidated by them
Into self censorship
The facility of his pen
He could not keep!

Ironically,
A mainstream press,
With a toothless face,
Rather conveys
An autocrat or,
To be precise,
A clinically-dead
Government in place!

A true friend

When my ambition
Hits its mark
Or when I am in black
No one shows me his back.

Many are at my disposal
For sure
So long as,
I have some to offer.

They bleed me dry
And away they fly.

When I am in the red
I have no one around.

A true friend
Without saying it goes
Remains close
Despite the test
The turn of events pose!

Acting bad to good end

Sometimes one has
To think out of the box
"Flog the workaholic ox
So that the indolent one
Dragged by the yoke
Willy-nilly , together, begins
To work!"

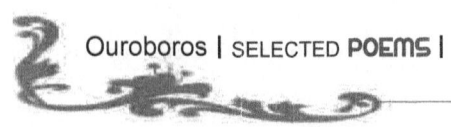

An ape's bald butts

It is when
It climbs up a tree
An ape's bald butts
Nitpickers can see.

Before having
The talent on hand
An upstart,one mustn't
Forge forward!

An honest despot

Donning a high flown
Robe of democracy,
Hypocrites barefacedly
Tout autocracy!

Alas,a snake
In the grass!

"Despot, if you
Serve as a jug and bottle
Or a parrot,
Materialize you could
Your wont.
Go ahead,
With a bloody iron fist,
Squash people's
Movement any,
To reshape
Their destiny!
For arresting

And deflating riot,
Worry not
About the armament,
Under the guise of
Aid to development
And rampant drought,
Succors to you
We shall underwrite.

With alacrity if you
Serve us
A Trojan horse,
And permit us
To siphon your
Country's resource,
We shall bless
Your reign
Of course!

To your
Petty acts
Of genocide
And corruption,

We shall give
Little or
No attention!
'The all-accounting court'
Must not cross your mind,
Rest assured it is not
For honest despots of
Your kind! "

Alas, a snake
in the grass!

"But as a man of
the people dear
To our dictates
Not giving ear,
If you try to err
From our road map,
If you attempt to flinch
An inch,
The holiness you preach—
In our nostril a stench

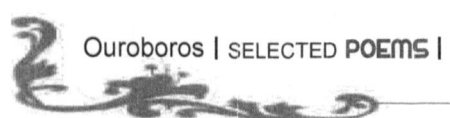
That itch—
Signals to us a conduct breach
Which begs for a pinch!

The democracy
We tailor out
Is a straitjacket
That keeps
With modern
Trends abreast,
Never try
To grow out of it
Don't be foolishly bold,
Do what you are told!
Don't you see
With your
Home-made outfit,
You look unkempt?"

"We hail from a special race,
Our linage to trace
Our ancestors were

Predators, slave owners
Colonizers and neo-colonizers!

Their successors,
We are globalizers- all-izers!
Thus we deserve
A higher place
In the power race!

You are not allowed
With us to catch up
And keep pace,
Slacken your defense,
Simply live by
Nuclear tappers grace!

Alas a snake
In the grass!

Lo and behold
The revolutions
The world
Watches agape,

Are shedding light
On the need
To change
The political landscape!
The fraternity and
Self-esteem spark
Freedom icons ignited,
We have to pursue united!

Freedom icons like Mandela
What is more Nkrumah
When we commemorate,
This let us not forget!

An overriding national feeling

Derartu, Haile, Tirunesh
Kenenisa, Meseret,Almaz and all
With a similar footfall!

Displaying a superb
Long-distance athletic feat
When many superstars
Awe-inspiringly you beat
And as a result of it
When your sought-for
Fought-for
And nation- prayed-for
Dream proves a hit
And also with kudos
A stadium full of people opt
You to greet
And when spectators
Accord you a high five

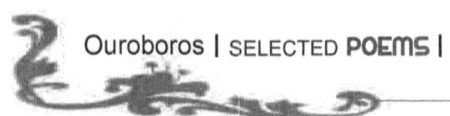
It is for your country's flag
You immediately dive!

Also on the podium
While Ethiopia's row-wise
Green, Yellow and Red
Emblazoned flag,
Shoulder high,
Soars above
You express
Your umbilical-cord-tight
National love
With tears that
Trickle down on each of
Your cheek, quick.

Is it because
Reminiscent of
Each living hero
With a life sacrifice
That brought colonial
Aggression to zero?

Is it because
The bounty of the land
You grew up
Seeing first hand?

Is it because
The cherished corner
You cut in the heart of
The poor but prideful
Ethiopian neighbor?

Is it because
The unity in diversity
That showcases
Ethiopia's identity
Or citizens hospitality?

Is it because
At heart strings a tug
Or, among others
Gratefulness to
Your iron-strong lung
When you hear
Ethiopian anthem sung?

Is it because
A secret another
Deep down you harbour?

Is it because
The fertility
Hope and
Sovereignty ideals
The flag advance,
Also Ethiopia's being
A beacon of independence
What is more
The nation's Renaissance,
Which before
A curtain of mist
Before your eyes dance?

Attention to its grotesque face

A ship sustaining
A tiny crack or thick
Is destined to sink,
Awaits the same story
A pilferers-leached country!

All the grotesque
Faces of corruption—
Embezzlement,bribery,
Red-tape,nepotism
Task procrastination
What is more inefficient
Resource utilization—
Must not go out of
A developing
Nation's radar,
Expected corruption
To bar

In its bid to spur
The ship of
Development far!

Needs no less attention
Fighting the new faces
Of corruption
Such as post placement
By political affiliation
Divorced from talent,
Which should enjoy
A greater weight!

Back to square one

That ethnic group,
A tyrant,
Was not a democrat!

On our right
For long it had
Indifferently squat,
Our throat,
Mercilessly it
Was about to cut.

Now, scenario's reversed,
The rein of power
We have gripped,
Democracy we have
Introduced!
To the follies
It made
In its heyday
It has to pay
Come on, on it
Sling a stone
The dark days
Had gone!

Bouncing back

Bouncing back
From cold shoulders
And many a rejection,
Resilient,I throw
My full weight
To get
What me await
In the storeroom
Of fate!

Bravo practice harmful traditions

In the far flung
Corner of the country born
There are tribal
Women, still, with ash
Cosmetic, red-soil
-made hair lotions
And plates inserted
In their lips
Themselves their way adorn!
When townees
Pay such women
A handsome money
To take their photo
Young girls follow suit
"Slit your lips
And insert a plate!"
As a motto!

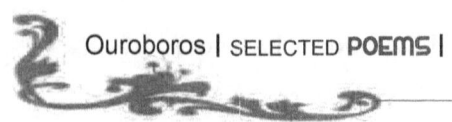
Breaking the double yoke

For ages
Saddled with
Domestic chores,
Confined indoors,
With a traditional muzzle
Devoid of a voice
With fellow housewives
We were sweltering
Under the class
And gender yoke
Seen weak though
We were hard a rock.

Things taking
A positive turn,
When people about
Women's potential
Came to learn,

Enjoying a level ground
And expertise,
As outshining
Women farmers
We have begun to enjoy
A handsome return.

After unremitting exertion
In a special way
Drawing attention
Investors we have indeed
Created job opportunities
For numerous in need
On their turn who have
Many mouths to feed.

We members of the fair sex
If not denied a chance,
Could outsmart
Many a man,in a given
Task,grappling with his part.

In the Science
And political arena
Ladies that prove brilliant
Must come to the limelight.

In the military
And peacekeeping task
On the athletics track,
There are also women
Who merit a tap on the back.

Breaking the double yoke
Must be the era's talk
Gender-based discrimination
Should no longer pose
In development's wheels
A spoke!
Let this volubly
Resonate from
North to South And
from Beijing To New
York!

By far better

S/he who openly loathes you
Is by far better than
S/he who covertly hates you!

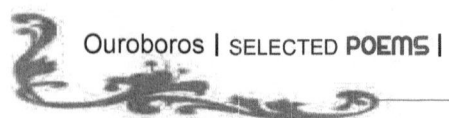

Cobra of the Arabian land

It holds high its head
Pursuant of a daily bread,
In a twinkle of an eye
Letting go the sand astray
Every which way
Cobra of the Arabian breed
Rips open the hot desert land
Turn twist,twist turn around
Underground
Till it catches
A lizard off its guard!

Come to Ethiopia

If nostalgia besets your mind
Come to Ethiopia
A cradle of mankind!

Come to Ethiopia
With no hesitation
Ancient civilization
Will engross your attention!

Before identity quest
You smother
Come to Ethiopia'cause
Lucy, your great,
Great grandmother
You could see closer!
A melting pot of
Over 80 ethnic groups who
With cordial hospitality,
Will embrace you
Without standing to ceremony

Or formality.
Come to Ethiopia
A mosaic of culture
A true place for adventure!

If you need
An original taste of
Coffee Arabica
Come to Ethiopia
A beacon light to Africa
To freedom fighters
Up to Caribbean Island
And America.

Come to Ethiopia
You will meet there
People who have to borrow
Valor from no where!

Come to Ethiopia
Triggering off no
Feelings of discomfort
Mosques churches abut.

Come to Ethiopia
In a way description
That defy a church
By a Muslim name goes by!

Come to Ethiopia
An exemplary country
To deter common enemy
To spur development
In a spectacular bent
Muslims and Christians unite!

Come to Ethiopia
Whose name on the bible
Times beyond number that does bubble.

Come to Ethiopia
For his persecuted
Followers,Prophet Mohammed
A safe haven marked!
Above all you will visit
Harar wall

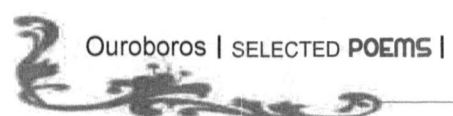
For world Muslims
The holiest city
On the row four!

Come to Ethiopia,
Now on the path of Renaissance,
Also mutual regional growth and
A sustainable peace
Are whose unwavering stance!

Come to Ethiopia
A country with its own
Alphabet and calendar!
Of course you will wonder
When you get yourself
Eight years younger!

Come to Ethiopia
To feast your eyes
On breathtaking water falls
Scenery and greenery
God-hand-made caves
Endemic animals and birds

Live volcanoes,
Obelisks and
Rock-hewn churches.
What is more
Konso terrace
And Ivangadi a spectacular
Traditional dance!

Come to Ethiopia
Aside from adventure,
You could collect
Invincible athletes
And successful Olympians'
Signature!
Your souvenir picture
With them you may capture!
Of course
You can board *Ethiopian*
That was there when
The horizon of
Aviation history
We scan.

Come to Ethiopia
The celebration of
The finding of the true cross
The pilgrimage
To Sheik Hussein Mosque
And epiphany
Have no parallels by any
On top of that
Thirteen months sunny!

Come to Ethiopia
To enjoy
A Teff-made
Flat bread organic
Found not carcinogenic!
You will gather
Like coffee
Teff and its bread chemistry
Time-old, with it,
That were there,
Are blessings
To the rest of the world
Ethiopia Proffer!

Come to Ethiopia
If you want to understand
As to what is meant
By a black pride!

If you worry
About class
Ethiopia today
Has hotels that outshine
With stars!
For global and
Continental organizations
A seat
For conference tourism
Ethiopia today is top on
The short list.

Congra to a dear boy

What a joy
What a joy
My little nephew,
Two decades back
Born abroad,
When a guest here
A ride on
A piggy shoulder
Who used to enjoy,
To whom I bought
A motley toy
Out of himself
Made a brilliant boy.

"As per my choice
Could you buy me a donkey
Or a could you allow me
A tortoise
To touch

When we go to
The squalid market square
Or the nearby church?"

Double mind
Is his nick name
Now crafting
Software is his game.

A small boy
Inquisitive
He used to ask
"Tell me why
Flowers don't grow
On the sky?"

"Tell me quick
Why animals
Don't speak?
Also stars
Don't grow

On the meadow?"

"Why is the sky high
To touch?"
Such questions helped him
Racking his brain
To come up with
Academic research,
That troubleshoot
Societal challenge
And afford
A nation a turnaround
Or for the better a change!

Now, conversant in IT
It is no wonder
To observe
Binary operation,flowcharts
Subroutines,syntax...
Programming languages
Are at the tip of his finger.

His study at
George Mason University
Has turned out a hit
Getting himself
In the Dean's List.

A boy that lends
To parents, relatives
And teachers
A heeding ear
Is really dear.

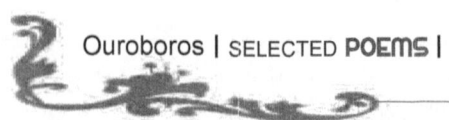

Crime by omission

Turning a blind eye
Also, intimidated to
Challenge the autocrats "Why?"
I condoned the slaying
Of the honest and workaholic
Subordinates on integrity's altar
Allowing on my conscience
An indelible scar.

Cure a wound another could

The desire to wholly
Posses you
Was so great
Bitter and harrowing
Was the feeling, unfaithful
To memory's dustbin
You relegate.

At a loss how
My problems to solve
Crying out my heart
By a serene cathedral door
My self to absolve
God blew on my way a dove!
With a tap on my shoulder
A sympathetic
And cute girl
On par with

My ex-lover
If not better
"Believe me
There will come
A time
You never recall
The heart sickness
Now you are
Taking tall!"

Cure a wound
Inflicted by a girl
Another could.

Devil could not be God

If willing
Their belief
On almighty
To relinquish
And from
Their soul
For lucifer
Proffer
A special dish,
For a while,
Devil will not be
Unwilling to grant
Sorcery and occultism
Blindfolded fools
The financial bonanza
They gluttonously wish
Or an earthly pleasure
They die to relish.

But at the height of
Their self contentment,
With a stab in the back
With a sharp knife
Satan will ramshackle
his subject's life.

Devil could
Not be God
However hard
he playacts
When approached
Ensconced on his abode.

Diameterically opposite mentality

Mother

My son is late to night
A bit drunk
He may be staggering in the dark,
God please return him back
Insulating him from thug's attack.

Wife

My husband is late to night
In a bar bewitched by enticing eyes
He may be inviting a tart for a dance.

Please devil throw him to hell
He is enjoying himself under a spell!

Different attitudes of mind

The innocent

By the sweat of
One's brow
Their likes aspire
To grow.
For them
Bread and water
Is all right
In so far as their walk
Could face the glare of light!

The corrupt

Bugs, they are not averse
To fattening
By the blood and tears of others!

Different faces of the same coin

Liberalizing democracy
To the extent of
Embracing perversion—
Going out of one's way
To promote sexual orientation—
Is no less transgression
Than strangulating it
With iron censorship—
Simply touting
The government
Is immaculate!

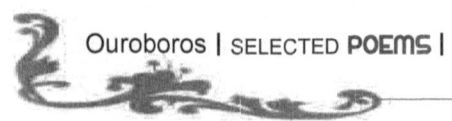

Different tongues of the same speech

Though they have
Different tongues
All religions
Have the same speech,
Peace,Love, Considerateness
And Hope
Are what each preach!

Is it not then
A glitch
Under the guise of religion
To teach
"Spell death!"
To s/he who has
a different faith!

Discharging inherited duty

Confused and fickle
I had been marring mine
And other's life to date
But this bent
I have grown to hate
So God
On my way blow
My soul mate.

Before the prime time of my lfe
Is gone
For my sins I have to atone.

As I observed
When it comes to delight
To looking after an offspring
Comes close nothing

Careless to forget
To procreate
Is a folly
I will live to regret!

Seconded is by none
To dads and moms
Seeing grandchildren.

Charged by parental
And a spouse's duty
I must discharge
Inherited by me responsibility.

Disciples of satan

As migrants workers in dire need of buttering their
bread
To Libya,the hardest way,some Ethiopians opted to
head.
They spent a portion of their life in a sweatshop
Clinging aloft a better-tomorrow hope.
Tragically, they were intercepted by ISIS members
with
A brain,inured,petrified and dead
After blood-thirsty, henious, ill-motivated and bad
shaped.
ISIS demons,who lavish atavism,ironically,the
faithful behead
With faith-based hatred.
Putting on a mask, they
Bullied 30 cross-necklace-bearing Ethiopians to a
desert shore,
Showcasing the brutality they adore—
The way a cat plays with
An inescapably captured rat—

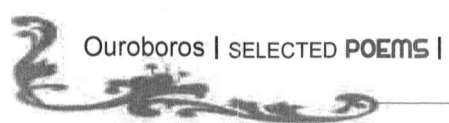

Rattling a saber at the kneeling down victim's back
Making sure their brutality to others prove stark
Like a a Hollywood movie they ordered 'attack!'
Oblivious
'Even slaying a sheep or a hen
Must be handled in a way that doesn't inflict a
pain!'

The Prophet's word ISIS members misconstrued
"The Muslim faith owes Ethiopian Orthodox a
gratitude!
So never attack a peaceful Ethiopian!"
What do they care,disciples of satan!
When an Ethiopian Muslim challenged them
"Where is your logic or reason?"
They shot him taking his act as a treason.

It is martyrs' souls that goes to heaven
While the unrepentant terrorists' souls
Are destined for hell's oven!

Distilling from the past making the future bright

Forefathers shedding blood
In a spectacular
Bravery and unity
Heralded
"A violated-not sovereignty
And self confidence"
For posterity!
What is more
An unpolluted culture
And intact identity!

Thus,maintaining integrity
And hard-preserved identity
Getting poverty and lack
Behind our back,
For the coming generation
We have to pave the track
With Mega projects Like
--GERD--
So that on a bright tomorrow
Our children embark!

Divergent paths

Though among
The chosen,
Judas of Iscariot
Opted to cross floor,
Out of his way
Heading to the path
Of the fallen!

In a spectacular way
Breaking loose from
The tight grip
Of the fallen,
Mary Magdalene braved
The arduous track
Of the chosen!

Heedless to a heavenly
Crown at hand,
Judas Iscariot hankered
For a monetary reward.
Giving attention

To soul's worth,
Mary Magdalene
Gave a red card
To her cherished perfume,
Though to procure it
She saved hard.

It was with a kiss
"This is He
You should not miss!
Now, as the given task is
accomplished Give me the 30 Birr
please!"
Judas betrayed Christ.
Repentant, while
Mary Magdalene
Washed Christ's feet
With tears.

Regretful Judas
Put a noose around his neck,
While, Mary Magdalene happily
Saw the resurrection of Christ
before a daybreak!

Do in Rome as Romans do

It should not come as a surprise
Though the right posture
A subordinate doesn't lack
"Do in Rome as Romans do!"
With a curved back
S/he has to walk!

It should not come as a surprise
Watching journalists
Praise that shower
On a tyrant government
In power!

Don't be a sheep in goat's age

A sheep and a goat once
Got locked in a fracas

"Off you go!
Don't you know
You are an embodiment
For an idiot!
How dare you trample
On the leaf, down
From the stem of an apple
That dangle,
And which I was apt
To cut and eat.

I really hate
A sheepish creature
Of your sort
With alacrity
To a dictate

Going to an altar
Is whose fate
And that no offense
On others inflict
Or none contradict.
A wet-blanket
A kill-joy
Or for the witty
A good toy!"
said the goat.

Dismayed and sad
The sheep replied

"In a futile bid
To satisfy your greed
With your horn blind
You scratched my feet
And began your complaint
To hoot.

Watch also what
You talk about
On doomsday

The likes of me stand
By the right of
The presiding judge
Jesus Christ.
While the likes of you
Cast to the left
Your lot
You shall lament.

An embodiment
Of the devil
Indulge in all evil
It is your wont
Oft to rebel
Also snobbish, than
Labor fault
In others to identify
Why don't you try
To see the bar
In your eye?
Horny got,I also wonder
How come you care not
Your private part
To cover!

You must not

Also forget
It is the addle-pate,
Who are prone all
To manipulate,
That call the
Poor- folk- in -Christ
An imbecile or
An idiot.

Though
'Don't be a sheep
In a goat's age!'
Is what is encapsulated
In today's adage,
You and I
Will never ever be
On the same page!

An Ethiopian
Will never ever
Change his skin,
Take note
Nor could
A sheep be a goat!"

Don't mistake me for a fool

When you find me
By choice cool
Mistake me not
For a fool.

If there is a need
For being cruel
I could over your eyes
Pull the wool
With out-heroding-herod's
Tool.

Unless imbeciles of your making
Get a first hand knowledge
What is meant by
A heart-overflowing-gal
Revenge
Or inflicted damage
As goes the adage

"A bull in a China shop!"
They gloat creating
Many a wreckage,
Harboring a grudge
They could never come to
The same page!

Double victory

My foe went down the pit
He painstakingly dug for me
To pitch down
Head first

•
   •
•
   •

V

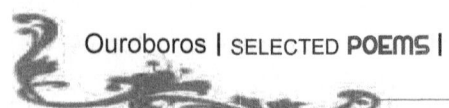

Duel of hearts

(A husband -> A wronged wife)

"My dear take a chair
Your affair is unfair
I can't stand
A suffocating air
This way you and I
Could no longer continue
A loving pair
Soon to my parents
I must repair!
How come
For love of a tart
A marital vow
You thwart?"
This way since
You decided me desert
For what I did spurred
By transient lust
Chagrin my soul has hit.
As usual in deep slumber

When I extend my hand
To ascertain whether
You have slept sound
And stir you up
So as we sleep entwined
Yet get awake to
A tragedy stark
That I but draw a blank
My heart indeed
Incessantly bleed
From the loss
It incurred
Your obeisance
And love divested.

If you can't find
It in your heart
My follies to forget
Forgive me my dear
For without you near
My life
Turns insufferably sour.
(A wronged wife—>A husband)

After your body
You befouled
And proved
A down to earth cad,
After your spirits
Perfidy you debased
Impudently you demand
As before
I should you hold
An esteemed husband.
Indeed this I will not!
For rancor laden my heart
Bleed incessant
It mustn't!
Away to my parents
I fled
For you failed to abscond
After what you did.
"Once bitten twice shy"
Forgive you how could I?
(A husband—>A wronged wife)
Your forgiveness but
Nothing depurate

The blot
In your eyes
Down me brought.
I hope
Forgiveness is the least
Your impeccable heart
Me could grant.
Even the ocean
Of tears I wept
Whitewash me still not
My dear
There is a second
Man goes wild
And commits a deed
He condemns absurd,
My perfidy
To nothing but
To this folly
Could be imputed.
Man is prone to err
So you should consider
What matters is his bid
Improprieties away to clear.

So my dear
Give me a chance second
To prove, you loving husband.
Your forgiveness
Will be a credit
That surely you catapult
To ensconce
In the apex of my heart.
A forgiving personality
Is a virtuous quality
Besides your heart
Me 'love' that taught
Which is also on me soft
Won't follow a policy
Watertight and
Once for all me smite
(A wronged wife—>A husband)
Raving and volleying
Boisterousness nay, nay!
You stultify
Must not I.
My mind is bedeviled

Since you I missed.
On your misdemeanor
Brood I shall no more
To night
Come to the cathedral
We first met
As a jump-start
Together out
We have to spend the night.
The night's zephyr wet
Will wipe away
Our disagreement!

Dust

When the water whirls
And whirls again
And gurgling when
It goes down the drain,
Forming a funnel,
The clay terrain
Caked on the bathing
Pool that does remain,
Conjures in one's mind
The excerpt," Man you are
dust and to dust
You shall return!"

Ego-rocking words

It will be futile
To gather you into my arm,
While my virility with
Ego-rocking words you harm!

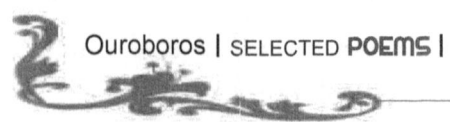

Elegy by a poet

Cold,closefisted
Gluttonous grave
Please release
My age-old friend
From gamboling fields
Schools, college
Working place
To blessed bed!

Cold,closefisted
Gluttonous grave
Please release
My wife and my life
My life and my wife
My love and my dove
My dove and love,
For my heart is her tomb
She leased with love
From her mother's womb!

Ethiopian winter

Splash
Rain,Rain and Rain
A sought-after
Ethiopian winter
Farmers are happy
To welcome you again
Tilling their land,
Select seed at hand.

Rain,Rain,Rain,
A tiny water ball,
Diagonally you fall
From high
When thunderous
Lightning plows the sky.
Though detested
Is your lash on
Townees' windowpane
Your tardiness
Is farmer's pain.

Rain,Rain and Rain
A seed sown on the sod
Takes bath in your hold
To give yields hundred fold.

Rain,Rain and Rain
Although you prove
Averse to a calm
Busy,a farmer
His wife and children
Know no rest
On the farm.
Porridge and hot drinks
Keeps them from
A befalling harm.

Rain,Rain and Rain
After allowing a shower
To crops, to a shiny sun
You cede place.
And when
The wind caresses
The crops at a mild pace

They exhibit
A choreographed dance,
Also with
A mellifluous music birds
From their nests
Forward advance,
While barefooted children
Run wild
No longer afraid
Of summer's dust whirlpool
Their eyes that blind
As lush grasses
Thrive here and there,
Agreeable, the occasion
Herds also find.

Rain,Rain and Rain
Till things
Shepard and herds get better
They retreat to a cave
Or in
A tree shade
Seek shelter.

Rain,Rain and Rain
Thirsty rivers inundate
Drank red-and-black-soils
Mixed water
To their hearts' content,
Making a confluence
To share to riparian countries
Ethiopia's blessings
And affluence.

Rain ,Rain and Rain
Neighbors,relatives
And friends
Cannot communicate
Also going to school
And a court
For two months
Comes to a halt.

Rain,Rain and Rain
When you depart,
Yellow daisies sprout!

Fear wedded life

I) A child
Though comfortably asleep
With a doll by my side,
Often I was terrified
A chimera could lurk
In the dark!
Also from a distance
When a dog bark
I saw it stark
A hyena with a horn
Was out
People to attack
Capable to pose Its
groutisque face
Behind my back.

II) A boy
Smote by a dream object
To anxiety I was subject.
As she was

Inaccessibly beautiful,
Self conscious,
I couldn't be cool
Terrifieed
"What if
Before her eyes
I prove a fool!"
Nor could I pursue the endavour
— Winning her heart—
'cause,topsy-turvey,to me
She turned an object of terror!

III) An adult
I was questioning myself
Whether "With my colleagues,
Could I rub a shoulder?
If not better."
"Compared with neighbors
Why,why,why
Financially I could not
Stand shoulder high?"

IV) A senior citizen

Putting under a question mark
My health
I kept on to ask
" To lustfully inherit
My wealth
My son or wife
Conspiring with
Heinous neighbors
Could spell my death!"
Enemies in the past,
What is more
The misdeeds of my wife,
Which were rife
Trailing by my mind
Bad days me remind!

Oft, with an ax
To grind
My self I find!

Fetching water with a sieve

Expect us not to believe
You could miraculously fetch
Water with a sieve!

Till we return to dust
You, nothing better than a rust,
Could not quench our thirst.

Collecting taxes
Without combing out lechers,
Who spare not even the broke
Or the stone to siphon,
Rather has an impact adverse,
For it is allowing few
Nation's wealth unfairly amass
At a cost of harm to
The credulous and
For-air-gasping broad mass!

Fidel(Faithful/Fiddle)

Tearing off
Imperialists' mantle
True to his name Fidel
He had lit
To the oppressed masses
And to those in the dark
A sought-after candle.

Weighing things from
Fraternity's angle
And the truth,
Like a sand dropped
On water forms a ripple
Fidel was not remiss
In dispatching own troops
In far off beyonds
To fortify for freedom
Mounted battle.

Considerate,
Fidel had taught

Innumerable orphans,
Whose combatant
Fathers lost.

Frowning up on amassing
Personal wealth,
He was building
The human power
Of the 3rd world
Like Ethiopia,
Among others,
In agriculture
And health!

Stooping to
Glittering things
While many leaders worried
To hanker for personal gain,
Fidel Castro,magnanimous,
Opted to assuage
The marginalized's pain.
For doing so
The shameless and bloodsucker

Imperialists were trying
To kill him again and again.
Yes, Fidle was their bane!

Though Fidel is no more
His legacy
Many shall live to adore!

Fight to the last

Though the future
Appears bleak
Don't yield to
Desperation quick,
Certainly there are
Other ways to pick.

Lamenting a lot
On your lot
Your wounds don't lick!
Don't nurse self-pity,
A luxury,
Which doesn't have
Use any!

Do what you can
With confidence
Leave the rest
To providence,
About the past

Which had already gone
Worry you should none
So far as there is no one
Who can undo
What has been done!

Fire balls

As I was walking through
The streets of Addis
With a mood very high,
Out of a clear blue sky,
A spark ignited by a pair of
Rolling big fire balls,
Affixed on either side
Of a straight nose,
Like a thunder
Unknown that falls
Threw open my heart's doors.
The spark embedded
In the embers
In my heart of
Hearts still lingers!

Fortunately it resuscitates

As mother nature's
Punitive measure
Against a society
In maintaining
The status quo
That doesn't bother,
Our rivers
Had become subject
To a water thirst,
To the extent
Of projecting rocky
Ribs terrifyingly
Protruded out
For easy count!

But now thanks to
The all-out,
Terrace making and
Reafforestation effort

Of each catchment
Farmers have made
A point
And also to
The afforestation
Move of the government
Rivers aside from
Quenching their
Insatiable thirst
Have resumed
To brim over
With floods
Drinking water
To their
Hearts' content.

Our forests
Once stripped of
Their wooded cover
Have started,
Fast, to recover
From afar
They are seen robed
Eye-catching green

From a frying-pan sky
Allowing a shelter
Also busy
Carbon to sequester.

Wild animals
That migrated
Have preferred
Back their way
To find.

Now, farmers
Don't have
Deep to dig
To sink
A water well
Or find
A nearby spring.

Birds are
Heard chirruping
Be it winter,
Summer or spring,

While brooks bubbling.

Buzzing and hovering
From this
To that flower
Bees are producing
Organic honey
By the hour.

Promising
A bumper harvest
Farmer's plots have
Fortunately continued
To resuscitate!
Those leaving their
Denuded abode behind
Away, who preferred
To stay
"We will return back
home soon!"
Is what
They say.

Happily enough
Mother nature affords
Us a second chance,
Imbued with
Environment stewardship,
If we are willing to mend
Our wrong
"Feast today
famine tomorrow! "
stance.

To dispel the specter
Of climate change
And systematically face
The global challenge
True to the adage
"We have either to
swim together
or sink together!"
Hence in fighting
The challenge
Or adapting
To the change,

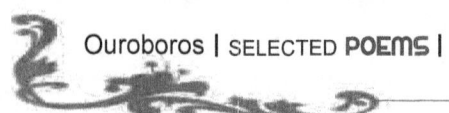
Back scratching,
We have to be
On the same page.

Indeed, irrigation must
Not slip our mind
For erratic rainfall
A lasting solution
If we must find.

Four hundred ninety

For a reason
I can't understand
Even after I extended
Them a helping hand
Also a good Samaritan
I shook off their dust
And pulled them up
From the sand,
There are people
Who do me
Things bad
Daring
"Do good to s/he
Who did you
Things bad!"
Topsy-turvy
On its head to stand.

But up on
A bit reflection

Something bubbles up
To my attention
Despite His
Benevolence untold
That is exactly what
I am doing on God.

Envoy

"Forgive
Your erring friend
Seventy times seven
If you want me

To welcome you
In heaven!"

Fresh two decades later

Although fate,
Distance and time
Cruelly put asunder
You an indifferent girl
And I a self conscious
Boy lover
Two decades later,
Lately,I saw you
A mesmeric lady
With a son
And a daughter,
Full of life
And laughter.

Once again
Your voice
In my cloud-shrouded heart
Rang a bell
To a paradise

That could
Change a hell.

Your sunrise
'I know you exist!'
smile
Still has power
Me, the cantankerous,
To beguile!

Alighting from
Ultra-modern car,
Transfixed,I saw you
Recede far!

From No where

My dear husband
If you were aware
Your love
Summoned me
From no where,
Suspect me
You wouldn't dare!

From the frying pan to the fire

Seeing a swarm of flies
Seeping the sap of
A hand-deprived
Leaper's fresh wound
A good Samaritanian
Disarrayed them with
A hand clap "Twa!" sound
Getting as close as he could
In vain expecting
"A thank you!" gratitude.

"You shouldn't have done that
When the former ones,
Who had their feels,depart,
The famished ones come forth
For their part
To siphon my blood
To their heart's delight!"

The upstart incumbent
Closed a curtain
On at the-end-of-the-tunnel-alluring light
Let alone warrant
The much-touted
Days bright—Democracy
Deepening
Across-the-board wealth sharing.

Revolutionary democrats
Who boast "Brave
In a guerrilla fight
We have sent
Tyrants to a grave!"
Serving the people
Opted to forget
So as
From government's coffer
To line up their pocket.
Tax-comafludged exploitation
Compounded by
Government-sponsored corruption,
What is more intimidation,

From one's land
Or abode alienation,
Exploitation aiming at
Ethnic cleansing,
Bureaucratic logjams
And maladministration
Creating hassle
Forums of non-stop discussion
From fever-pitch
Brewing up political tension
To divert attention
Are the tactics
They use
To sustain
Their tenure
And advance
Bad governance.

Gambled wrong

When you let
Your paramour
Eat me out of a room
I rented in your heart
Prior I became
Your bridegroom,
Forebode,your liberty,
A predicament
A marital earth-quick,
Divorce!

So be it
Walk down the aisle
With your paramour
And behind me
Slam the door
Ashore, a wrack
Brushed aside
Pensive,love
To passion
Is exchanged,

Averse to the
Tragic drama
That does unfold
My tails
Amid my legs tagged
Away shall recede
I, the jilted.

But make note
My dear,
If you dare
To barter a
Husband for
A paramour
The paramour
Husband turned
Will question
For sure him
Whether you
Genuinely adore
For,if for him
You can steal
Steal from him
You will.

God couldn't be wrong

Indefatigable
In her task
Carrying her baby
On the back
A
drudgery-saddled-and-lactating
mother often embark
On fanning the ember
Into a spark.

Before she
Puts a dish
On the stove, Assuming
all glittering Is worthwhile to
relish,
Her child may wish, Over her
shoulder Stretching his hand

To grab
The red-hot charcoal,
Mistaking it
For a lovely red ball!

Thus he wails
When forced
His Pandora-box wish,
To relinquish!

So also when checked
Unhampered not to surge
Ahead to victory's door
We aspired for,
We must not blame God
For He might be
Shielding us from
A misfortune the
Future holds in store,
Or a pitfall untold
Down the road!

God could be never wrong
Firm in belief all along
The rocky journey
Life-long
We have to praise Him
With a gracious song!

When we get
Or not get
For what we long
Also know we must
God has his own
Timetable—
Say to surprise us
With a windfall apple
Or to make
The single a couple!

Great tiding

Blue Nile echo from shore to shore,
'Poverty in Ethiopia is no more!'

Above all,
From a precipice
To a valley when you majestically fall,
Thunderous over
The damp dell, mountain gorge when you roll,
As usual
With green, yellow and red
Rainbow arched,
Tell Ethiopia loud-
"Your children you very much adore,
A lip service they now abhor!
'Blue Nile has no lodging,
Yet it loafs a log hauling.'"

Blue Nile, about your deeds to talk
Breathtaking, you served well
The industry without smoke,

But now you have an extra work!

       Far

           And

              Wide

          Ethiopia will be electrified,

With Blue Nile,

      Gebe &

              Tekeze... at hand!

Every nook and cranny will get light,

When efforts Ethiopians unite!

The future will be bright,

When a tamed Blue Nile ceases

Unchecked to roar past

Without a respite.

No energy source runs waste

Nor any Plant will suffer a blackout!

Lo and behold Blue Nile will be subdued

For riparian countries' good!

To contribute a brick,
Ethiopians twice you shouldn't think.
Farmers have mounted on a peaceful battle,
To cover the catchment with a green mantle,
To make terrace
On each mountain
Taking every pain.
To afforest the depleted f o r e s t!
Thus washing on its way,
Blue Nile conspires no more
To carry alluvial soil away.

Here, of course, it is good to recall
The message of Emperor Twedrose.
'Dear guests you are
Amid people hospitable,
Welcome, welcome
Feel at home!
Roam throughout
Abyssinia you might,
On its grandeur your eyes
You can feast.

The vast array of
Mouthwatering dish,
The country parades
You could relish.

In case you wish
For an adventure,
Still Ethiopia
Is a mosaic of culture!

Of course
It will grab your attention,
Ethiopia's being
A cradle of mankind
And ancient civilization.
You will see
To its music heart titillating,
Comes close nothing!
Moreover fails not
To draw your attention,
The affection
Among people hailing from
Different nationalities and religion.

But you can't transport a speck of dust,
Alighted or pasted on your shoe by accident!
So to get an exit,
Shake off your shoe and wash your feet!

Giving to every dust attention
It is possible to ward off
The problem of silt accumilation.
Besides don't you think
The forests serve a carbon sink?

Blue Nile echo from shore to shore
'Poverty in Ethiopia is no more!'

As though Abyssinia,
Africa's water tower
Is a weakling with no power,
On every news hour,
Portraying Ethiopia
A development backwater,
Also scornfully on a dictionary
Painting its people thirsty and hungry
Have no grounds any!

From a rain-fed agriculture
Head on
Making a paradigm shift,
Irrigation when Ethiopia further adopt,
The vicious cycle of drought,
Which pose a threat
To its development,
Will give way to a bumper harvest,
Once more rendering Ethiopia
A cornucopia.

Ethiopians be not cool,
Be not cool
Resources to pool!

Lo and behold Blue Nile will be subdued
For riparian countries' good!

Yet, yet hanging up together
Be high on the alert
Any aggressor to deter!
Many are
Who wear a frowning face,

When development
In Ethiopia picks pace!

Keep open your eyes,
Keep open your eyes
At all time, all space
Where infrastructures
Are put in place.
To the helm of development
Ethiopia will soon catapult
When its children
In full harness their resources put.
So cognizant of this fact,
Ethiopians allow not
The grass to grow under your feet.
Don't wait
Behind the campaign
To throw your full weight!

For work, roll up your sleeve
Ready for 'The Renaissance Dam'
Your sweat

B

L

O

O

D

And life to give.

March out for prosperity

In Ethiopia to thrive,

What we need have

Is a bond-cohesive

A

:

B-O-N-Decisive.

Go all out, go all out,

Us, lucky we have to count

For seizing such a ripe moment.

Blue Nile echo from shore to shore

'Poverty in Ethiopia is no more!'

Come on let us not beg to differ,

Of course we could concur,

For all of us will agree,

Our pet dream is to see,
Ethiopia industrialized
Completely transformed!

Laying the foundation,
Where on takes off
The future generation,
Is what begs for
Central attention.
Why, Why and Why,
With our hands
Tucked in our pockets,
You and I
Remain standers by?
Also why
Simply watch the clouds
Glide across the sky?
Must we indeed,
Sowing a discord seed
Allow our rivers run wild,
Turning a blind eye to our need.

Wiseacres, though
You may not be on the same page,

Between stakeholders
Don't drive a wedge.

In life it is not hard
To get skeptics,
Our leaders talk your walk
Walking your talk!
Prove skeptics wrong
Letting them witness
The actualization
Of the dam agog.

Also we need
Target rent seekers
That drive spokes
In to development wheels.

See any tax arrear
Finds its ways to
The government's coffer.
Taxes being
A development backbone
Must be mysterious to none.

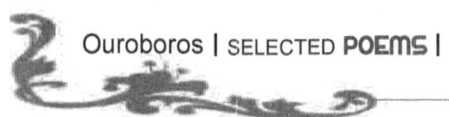
Had I not

Had I not relished
What I had long cherished
Had I not tasted
And grown out of
What success has in store
Going past its door,
I would have
Squandered my life
With a carcinogenic self pity
For failing to cross floor.

Have you visited your brother in need?

Though barely clad,
He was fully attired
With chocolates of mud,
Which even pasted
A leg-burrow
Of a small
Walking scarecrow,
What a sorrow!

A sore-eyed
And malnourished child
That developed
A leg bandy
'Cause buckling from
A pot-belly
Subject to ailments every
Prominently Kwashiorkor
And scurvy

By twist of fate
Pushed out
To the street
To sleep he used
By every bus-stand,
An orphan boy,poor,
Showered with
A heavy downpour!

A biting cold untold
With a face
Smile wrinkled
He weathered,
Despite an urge
For a morsel of bread.

A dog rabid, moreover
He was chased
From every nook and corner!

Mixed with boys of his kind
From the street
For freedom with a bent,

One night
To the bone chilled
By a cold wind
On the morrow dead
He was found!

The sought-for warmth
He acquired in his death!

Yet fellow citizens
Are busy to take note
To hundreds of his sort!

It is surprising indeed
No one gives a heed
To the challenge of God
"Have you visited
Your brother in need?"

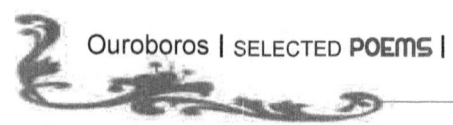
Heroines in the dark

Though it is good
To bring to the limelight
Women brilliant,
In different walks of life
Who fought their way
To inaccessible height,
We must not forget
Starving-and-
drudgery-saddled mothers,
Who their children
To school send
With full stomach,
Too deserve
A pat on the back!
This must be also
Included in our talk
Specially when March 8
We mark!

How then?

Why my dear
When laid I my eyes
On you first,
Heart mine
In my throat
An asylum sought?

Why my dear
When my ear
Fine-tuned got
To your voice
Dulcet
Out of me
I jumped out?

Why my dear
For instance
Your scent
Of a rose fragrance
I inhaled,

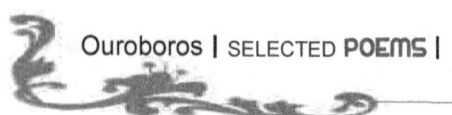
Perched I remained
Than alive more dead!

Why my dear me
When you first greet
My tongue
Oft adept
Twice as much
To reverberate
Panic gripped slept?

How then
My dear,
Fidgeting,
I to you
Me endear?

How to tell a fool

A snake bites a fool twice
"It is this one that stung me once!"
To show when he makes advance.

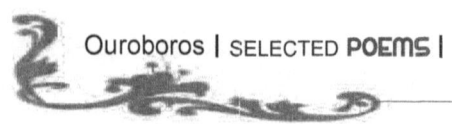
I can't help asking

Three decades back,
A communist,
As a fad atheist,
To my chagrin
You taught us
"God doesn't exist!"

With dropping jaws,
After mass
I saw you yesterday
Kneeling down
Hands upward
Wholeheartedly when
You pray.

Out of His mercy
And benevolence,
No doubt,
God will forgive you
At once,

For what matters
Is your repentance.

But I can't help asking
What will be the fate of
Those credulous children,
At their formative years,
You sent off the track
Without a mental map
To return back?

Inequalities of all shades

Though in dexterity
My physically challenged
carpenter-father,
Than the physically fit
Proves better,
As a source to his anger,
With contemporaries
A level ground
He enjoyed never!

From late childhood,
There was one thing
That me used to bother,
Why my so
Discriminated father
On his turn
True to cultural dictates,
Ill treats my domestic-
chores-saddled mother

And heeds not her say
Though by
The sweat of their brow
As responsible parents
They were happily bringing up
My sister and I together?

I still wonder
Why, why, why
My sister, who has IQ
On par with me
If not better,
To help out mother,
Suffering a cold shoulder
Even by her Mom,
Was denied the right
To pursue education further
While I was given a chance
To prove a man of letter(s).

I remember,
Crossing many a pool,
Barefooted,I used to trek
A long distance to

A nearby town's school,
Where for my provincial
And shabby clothes
I was seen a fool
By the relatively rich
In showing courtesy
Far from cool.
Though stationery
They didn't lack,
Sad,I had a hand
Tied behind my back.

Alas, up on
Joining campus
Where I yearned for
The sagacious a chance
There too in my class,
I was looked down
By students
Hailing from families
Of the top brass.

When I went abroad

For a higher education
Enjoying fellowship
And donation
Worse still,I met many,
Color has colored
Whose vision.
Ironically,
My dissertation was
Drawing attention
To why should
The broad mass be
Standers by
And with ill-fate
Marked die,
While the favored,
Racist
And the corrupt few
Gobble over
About 3/4 of the pie?

Is capable to mar

With your sweet lips,
On which oft
I yearn to plant a kiss,
Slander me not please!

My lodestar
You must know
A drop of gal
The wellspring of honey
Is capable to mar!

It could buy the priceless life

Though life is priceless
And invaluable,
To be frank,
The blood, one donates
To a blood bank,
An oasis in
Life-devoid desert
A delivering mother's
An accident victim's
A nation defending
Soldier's life
Helps to regain back!
What a lofty task!
What a lofty task!

Donating the resilient
Blood does not affect
Our health's Status quo,

So once in a while
Let us learn, to a nearby
Blood bank to go!

When sinks in the idea,
Of such a holy venture
Following suit,
All will nurture
The culture!

It is meant for one

When smiles
From my teeth
You often scan
Do not conclusion jump
Own my heart you can,
The former is for all
But the latter for one.

Keeping distance

Though keeping
The necessary distance
I often retreat,
Missreading
My sagacious move
As a defeat
Upstarts began,
Going out of their way
On me damages to inflict!

Nudging me out of
My shell,
They adore
Turning my life
A hell!

Lacerating is the pain

Love of my life
The knowledge
We are on the ball
Makes me take pride
And walk tall.

Even if
About me
You know all,
Try to understand
The problem
On my side,
Every time,lacerating
Is the pain
Parted,till
I get you again!

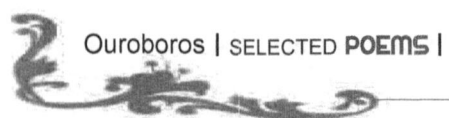
Let Us Leave Divide And Rule For The Fool

Gripped by fright
A full-scale fight
Could once more breakout
At any moment be it
Day or night,
The cousins Ethiopia
And Eritrea
Were beefing up
Their military might
Locked in a border dispute
Exacerbating border
Inhabitants' plight.

For long,
Leaders of the horn
And the international community

204

Had been observing developments agog
Forced to tune
To the cacophonous war song
"In military prowess
I am the one strong!
A rabbit, I will hack you
Like a feral dog!"

In such shows of force
There was not
Squandered not resource,
Which could feed
Innumerable needy, of course.

In a paradigm shift

"Among siblings
If reign supreme must
Considerateness and peace,
For a border dispute
There is no room please.

Let us build a bridge

Not a wall
Towards common growth
The strife-ridden Horn
Must get on the ball.

True to the court's
Binding verdict,
President Isaias
Take Bademe as a gift.

To the confluence
Adding up
Is the new roadmap!'

"Thank you Prime Minister
Dr. Abiy
If love and developmental
Thrust are entailed
In the roadmap
Rest assured,
I will accord
Your gesture
Thumps up.

Yes, we have to leave
Divide and rule
For the fool!
If the horn
Is to get on the ball,
Add up must all!"

Liberating the mind before the land

From formative years
To adulthood serfs-baited
Modern slaves ill-treated
From their means
Of existence alienated,
It is with hatred
From- serfdom- of- every
-kind-the- newly -unshackled
heads' formatted!

Though their
Much-lamented land
Had come back to their hand
Tardy, their mind
Proves not free,
That is why they engage
In a killing spree!
Worse still, death to all
Allies inclusive,they decree!

Although it sounds funny
They pay back gal
For received honey!

Also to cultural norms
And religious ideals blind,
Atavistic they slay
A woman and a child
In a way that is wild.

Oblivious for 9-months
They had a lodging
In a mother's womb
They want to blast it
With a bomb!
They want to shove in it
A spherical thorny wood
As far as they could.

Alive, they grill a man,
For idle or unskilled what
They can't do, he can!

In the name of God
Or religious sects,
Replete at this
Satan-released age,
They behead a man
Created in God's image!

Licking one's own blood

Eskimos bury
The handle of
A razor-sharp knife,
Bearing a lump of
Frozen meat, to be precise
Layers of blood in the wilderness of ice.

Lured, wolfs gather round it
And unaware their own
Snow-frozen tongues they slit
They voraciously lick, lick and lick
Along with own blood, hot and tick.

'What a windfall luck!'
They think
'We are feeding on our blood!'

Before comes to their head
They find themselves dropping dead!

Hankering for personal gain
Blindfolded by gluttony
There are citizens who
Government's coffer drain.

With the wrong mindset
'We are smart and brave'
They push their country,
Their foothold or abode,
To a grave!

Like a cigarette

Bro,tell me please
To your heart's content
Enjoying a French Kiss
In squeezing out
The nectar of their
Lady-hood not remiss,
Are the lasses
Just like a cigarette
For a while you keep
By your chest
To burn them to ashes
And ignominiously
Squash them down
Under your heels?

Like a moth to a flame

Myself I have to blame
After declaring
"I have severed
Our relation
Intolerant to
Her theatrical-
and-self-seeking
Love game!"
Back to square one,under
The pretext of sympathy ,of course,
Buckling under her sight and voice
I acted the same
Like a moth to a flame!

Though my siblings and friends
Advised,
"A leech,except parasitizing
She has no other intent!

Hence,inconsiderate
She will bleed you dry
Why should you call her my dove?
'Cause her sentiment is far from love,
Dump her,the problem to solve!"
Back to square one,
Under the pretext of
Evading a conscious-pang—A fickle—
I acted the same,like a moth to a flame!

Offence-blind ,proving a fool,
I failed to see the wide room
For her to be unfaithful!
No sooner we got out of bed,
Acid to my salary,
Though to garner it
Back myself I have to bend,
She used to hand it over
To her indolent boy friend!
Though I knew
Our love was clinically dead,
My youthful life on
A bitter love
I was forced to spend!

Lock me in a debate

Least conscience mine
Intermittently me smite
Alluding to the follies
And guilt impetuously
I plunge steadfast
And which to memory's getho
I toil to relegate,
Lean,I must on someone
Who nonstop
Locks me in a debate
Or a task
That gives me no rest
Even an alcoholic solace
That lends my head
A fanciful flight
Rendering my
(Guilt-laden)
Conscience dormant!

Loss amplifies the merit of the missed

A sudden power outage
Rams home
Light's advantage!

What exactly is meant
By inexorable grief,
Dawned on me
Off my guard
When you
Turned brief,
Setting my heart afire
With anguish
That knows not a relief!

What a blind nose
That doesn't sense
Death hovers close!
That is why

Oblivious to facts
On the ground
I stuck to
"Forever together!"

Yet, happily
The Almighty lends
The bereaved power
To outgrow
Such a gloomy hour!

Love

Love is not
By fair means or foul
Meeting one's end,
But it is
The negative good
Care to the beloved
Is ensured!

Love has a timeless appeal

A faded rose
Retains its
Fragrance for the nose!

At a train station
Something exemplary
Drew my attention
I saw an old man
Kissing his aged wife
"Love of my Life!"

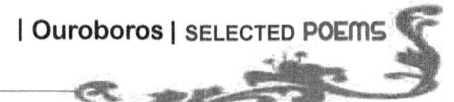

Lovely

Befriending hundred girls smart
Doesn't afford half the delight
As catching your sight!

Luck is what I lack

Lack is not
What denied me luck
Rather luck is what I lack!

Yet I craft poems a lot
To change my lot,
God willing,
One day to hit
A poetry-contest jackpot!

Mandela the moral giant

Intoxicated with
"Might is right!"
The moral dwarfs,
With beefed up muscles
And iron fists,
Drove home fright
Killing and leeching
Alienated natives
Day and night!
They brutally
Subjugated many,who
With bare hands,
For God-given freedom
Have to fight!

Up on gaining
Back freedom,

Revolted by

"An eye for an eye!"

Mandela the moral giant

Declared

"Retaliation what for

and why?

A moral dwarf, like

Ex-bosses,

Degrade myself must I?

Though I was robbed of

Sunlight from a lullaby

Almost to the day

I die!"

" 'The peace

and considerateness'

Placard is what we must

Worldwide hover high!

All of us are

On our way out

So, let us make sure
Behind us we leave
Days bright!

Also, we must not forget
Among the white
The presence of
The moral giants,
Who fight for
Blacks' right!"

Mistake me not for a fool

When you find me
By choice cool
Mistake me not
For a fool.

If there is a need
For being cruel,
I could over
Your eyes pull the wool
With
Out-heroding-herod's tool.

Unless imbeciles like you
Get a-first-hand knowledge
What is meant by
A gal-overflowing
Heart's revenge
Or inflicted damage

As goes the adage
"A bull in a China shop!"
They gloat creating
Many a wreckage,
Harboring a grudge
They could never come to
The same page!

Monkey's Mentality

With an intent of
Stripping of all-wives and footholds-
And taking over
Measuring father's footmark
Walking behind father's back
A monkey inflicts on the same attack
Cognizant,subject to
The wear and tear of time,
Feeble,
A defensive hand
The father could lack!

A mentor, I helped
An apprentice
Acquire a sharp mind
And a nimble hand
Till on his feet stand.

When he realized
He has ensured balance
Began the apprentice
Forward advance,
Quite strange to the behaviour
Of other apprentices,
Ungrateful,he started to hurl
Acerbic remark
About my skills,
Casting a covetous glance
For boss's chair a chance.

Moral

Moral is a hydra
That has a head extra!

Must she be like
a fairy-tale princess?

Though from fairy-tale
Princesses less attractive,
Many a man fails
To notice
A quality love
She could give
As much as
She could receive.
Admiring her
Internal beauty
Compensated by
Her faithfulness,
Integrity and honesty
Adored by her
Enjoying a marital bliss

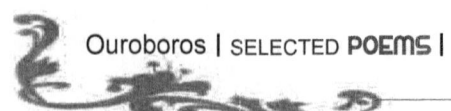

It is a fortune
Long with her to live!

Must your gratitude be a knife?

On top of my labour
In the farmyard
I often proffer you
Milk, cheese, manure
And hide
To render grand
Your life,
Then how come
You express
Your gratitude
With a knife?

My daughter

Of all things,
The very idea of
Going to school
Drives my daughter
Into tears.

When I beg her
There to go
She always says "No!"
When I tell her
If you prove such a bore
"I could no longer
You adore!"
She cries all the more.

Afraid "Spare the rod
And spoil the child"
I hint to her a walloping
She cries "I am not going!"

When the incident
At a work place I recollect,
The admonishment
My daughter I dealt
Rends my heart.
Admonish her I have to yet
For otherwise
She will be
A spoiled brat!

My princess

A warm morning sun
Flickering a ray of light
Making my fogy
Bachelor's heart bright,
A curtain raiser
Thawing the ice
Of solitude
You afforded me
A turnaround
That rendered
My life sound.

What a surprise
You gave me children—
God's gifts at His
Own guise!

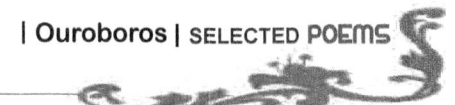

Newton's fourth law

The back and forth motion
Will produce a lotion.

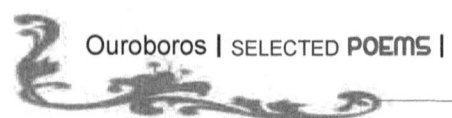
No compensation

No compensation will atone
For the gruesome betrayal
One had undergone
Languishing under
Soul's dark night alone!

No condom no sex

(Sex Worker to a house wife - >)

Entertain not for me hatred
It is only for a daily bread
I take your husband abed.

Since you are so timid
In haste,you leave your husband
Restless and discontented.

Lovemaking is an art
My dear sister
You should surely master
Than on me nicknames pester
Harlot, Slut, Hooker and a Whore!

Read a lot on the subject
With your spouse develop the art
At long last
When you prove your dexterity

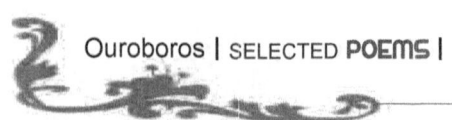

In conjugal felicity
A tip it would be for mental integrity.

With affection and suggestion open
Your spouse, you can turn
A love-making machine,
What else do you need in return.
By the by
You may not seek a hit on the sly.

(<- A housewife to a sex worker)

My dear sister in Christ
I know there is nothing
Foul in your heart
Except, you are
A sex worker by ill fate.
Thanks a lot for your comment
Which I will second no doubt.

Dear sister in Christ
At times if both
You and my husband
Get debouch of beer or Highland

Check you have a condom at hand
Just when you hold him inside,
For otherwise
Severe will be the consequence
For me and my child.

So you are morally obliged
By 'No Condom no Sex!' to abide
I am also willing to you extend
A helping hand
That could help you
On your feet stand
Than your flesh trade
For a daily bread!

No rose with out a thorn

To pluck an eye-catching rose
One risks a piercing
It could pose,
Though lovely,it is prickly!

Even if fully attired
With beauty,
She is a bit naughty!

Old Flame

Though irretrievably
We had missed the boat
And in the meantime comfort
From many a consort
I did sought,
Still your substitute
I haven't got
From the lot
Fate's wind
On its sway has brought.

Yesterday's old flame
Had conveyed to me
The same!

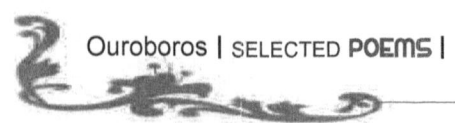
On the frying pan

Unzip a snow-white teeth
A popcorn can
On the frying pan!

Confronted by
Circumstances dark,
I learned, with optimism,
Crushed spirits and strength-
sapping moods to mask.

Adopted I
Relegating gloomy things
To memory's back!

On the wrong heart

When a kid
I used to put
My boot
On the wrong foot!

A grown up
I put trust
On the wrong heart!

Opted to escape

Before I got me
Back in shape
Life's unilateral
And busy train
Opted to escape.

Opted life to escape
While I was
Dreaming about
An elixir
Or some sort of help!

Ouroborous

Ouroboros is its own meal
The same is true with
Those from own country
That steal!
To hamstrung the incumbent
Most party members
Are not hesitant.
Ouroboros, they adore
Their party,
Which they obliviously or
Otherwise sully with
A rent-seeking identity.
They adore the incumbent
Yet they spell nation's
Slow but sure death
Siphoning budget earmarked
For infrastructure, education,
Agriculture and health.
They adore their party
That took power

But with a dead face
Tolerate them, with
Nation's wealth,
Take a shower.
They adore their party,
However with
Their bureaucratic logjams,
Create on nation's developmental
Thrust encumbrance.
Yet they entertain
A wild dream
Their party could
Let the country
Forward advance.
They support their party
As a scare (self-defeating) tactic
Sees better
For social justice
Requesting demonstrators
To scatter
Gunning down one or two
With a sniper.
'Cause what they enunciate

'We adore'
Audiences abhor
Marking it
Stifling and 'a bore'.
Worse still,
Barefaced they entertain
No shame or fear
Using 'public media'
'I kill thee
Because I love thee!'
To din in people's ear.

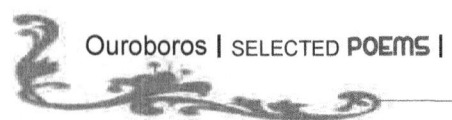
Out of bed four

Absurd it is indeed
Brought together
By life's tide
Husband and wife pronounced
We sleep entwined,
Yet, our dreams disarrayed
Also by diplomacy
Masked our rancor
We get out of bed four!

Patricide

When a patricide was
Brought to my attention
As saw fit tradition
I vowed to take even.
Vindictive of my patricide
Going to my homeland
With a hatchet at hand
Every barn,forest and farmland
In vain high and low I searched
The nook that seemed deserted.
Undaunted yet desperate
When to a neighboring village I went
Wistful in a tree shade squat
With a hair completely white
An old man me beckoned
This to impart
"It is from a homicide hunger born
For good to heaven
Your father relatives
And Neighbors gone.
Bury the hatchet

Stop the past to lament
And with a hoe dig the land!
And harness the rivers
That flow unchecked
Water the scalded land
Afforest the barn land
It is only then and then
The score to your patricide
You can even
For hunger your patricide
Is by its very nature a different
With a hatchet
A tie could hardly be dealt.

Preposterous

To the natural course preposterous
As a brook upstream that gushes,
To self-consciousness averse,
I shake me hands
When I dip my diffidence
And doubts
In liquor bottles!

Proves good

A freezing celibacy
Proves good
Than an intimacy,
In no time that
Tumbles
As a pack of cards!

Psychological dome

Forcing passers by
Curious for peep stand,
Swelling a throng
By every square
Or a roadside,
Using his right leg
A nimble right hand
With the other holding
The artifact items hard
A handless man
Makes attractive tablets
And tools
Hammering nails
And cutting woods
The way the task demand,
A task, many normal people
Imagine, to handle hard.

Those who appreciate
His talent
Throws coins —

A tip for his pocket,
While some buy
The artifact items
He puts up for market.

Aside from eking out
A living
He hits home
The psychological dome
"Disability is not inability!"

In a similar case,
An art mentor
And an apprentice
Draw many a
Wonderful picture
With his mouth
The latter
In a manner
Attention that capture
Hitting home "Some qualities
If deprived by mother nature
Other qualities man could nurture!"

Queen of my heart

By a girl description past
Smitten,say more I can't
She is mesmeric and exquisite.

The most exquisite
Under the sun,
Top on the sky,
In the rank of beauty
She stands high!

Eve is what she goes by
This beauty incarnate and
Feast of the eye!

Whenever Eve passes by
She pales the charms of all
Who are out their luck to try.

As the days go by
All flowers wilt and die,
Yet Eve blooms

In my very eye!

Eve shines bright
Winter, summer,day and night
I wonder she is crafted in what art,
My dearest rare sight!

Eve my little rose bud,
The world has never witnessed
A flower
With splendor so attired.
Afire eve set
My heart's cresset
When I catch her sight.

Off my feet I was swept,
The very moment's
Her gaze
I chanced to intercept.
Who I may be
An eye she never bat!
Yet she is in the
Cherished corner of
My heart
Hope, light, delight

And queen to it.

If eve hear my cry
I want her to be
Inviolably my,
And oft I die
To walk by her,
Shoulder high
Ever with alacrity
Her dictates to abide by.

My longings
Will linger longer
Till I materialize
My desire!

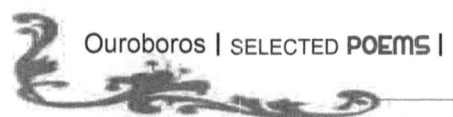

Quite strange

Finding ourselves
No longer two,
I and you
Set a plan
To prove
One plus one
Is one.

But, averse to what
Arithmetic decree
We ended up
One plus one is three!

Realizing his kingdom

Foolishly bold
Abnegating God
To get attention
Famous by
A negative association
Is moral degradation.

The beginning
Of wisdom
Is realizing
His kingdom.

Regretted I

When I heard today
Your passing away
Regretted I
Failed to pay
You a visit why?

Regretted I
Why, why, why, why
Failed to say goodbye
On your sickbed
Looking at your eye?

Regretted I
Told you not why
Your kindness and honesty
Were descriptions that defy?

Submerged in life's
Rest-not-knowing chores
Oblivious, I was of course!

Remiss in expanding

The mouth of the pit,
For a frog stranded in it,
Is the sky's limit!

Displaying reluctance
To expand mental horizon
That strengthens
Their stance,
Disputing permeates
Their parlance!

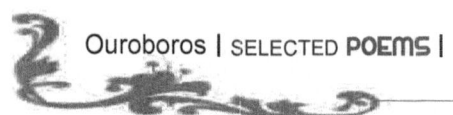
Revamped

Home, when I repair
The day's drudgery
Rolled over
"Hurrah,
Daddy has come!"
When my children cheer
Banging the door,
Bathed with smiles
When my wife,
A pillar of my life,
A kiss on me confer,
And also
When we say a prayer
Sitting for dinner,
Revamped I turn
For a drudgery
In store!

Sandwiched in between

An unforgettable
Memory to cherish
A glimmer of hope
To relish
Renders life, sandwiched
In between,
A sumptuous dish!

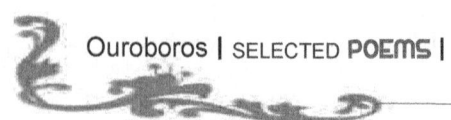

Season's king—
Spring

Welcome,welcome Spring
Freedom of movement
In one's mind ring.
Birds that adore to sing,
Also for
Nectar-buzzing
Bees are on the wing,
While brooks keep on bubbling.

Welcome,welcome Spring
You stamp on everything
Uplifting mood
On hibernating animals
And each wood.

Earth rolls out
A yellow daisy carpet
Embroidered by

Flowers vintage,purple
And violet,
To a blue sky
Its pet.
Rabbits and insects of every kind
Salubrious the occasion find.
While parents on
The departed season
Take a stock,
Children on the gamboling fields
And football pitches run amok
Unless checked round the clock
From the nearby forest fruits boys pick
"This one has a cover tick
That one is toothsome,while this mouthwatering.
Try this to eat, it is bitter sweet!"

In pairs,lover shepherds and firewood fetching girls
Head to a close by mountain,
To quench thirst from love's fountain.
Swimming and washing in the pool,
Students get ready to start school.

With full granary , adults throw innumerable party
Turning humorous and funny
They turn by turn ask each others' company
To their children's wedding ceremony.
They sing,dance, dance and sing
Appreciative of seasons' king—SPRING.

Seduction

Awakening and rekindling
The exhilarating experience
Of being a cherished object
Of love and desire
With a flattering affectionate look
"Other than you I have
No beauty to admire!"
Fanning the ember of
An emotionally not-checked-in
Wife's lady hood in to a fire
He put off her attire
To enjoy a forbidden fruit
He never imagined
He could succeed to acquire!

The girl who shunned him
Preferring a filth-rich man,
After a lot of water
Passed under the bridge,
This way, he began to man

Though suffering a conscious pang
That he has turned
A disciple of Satan.

But he is bold
With his chest to parry
A bullet shot towards the one
A beauty he behold.

She looked him askance

He showed a cold shoulder
To a dove,
Who was yearning
For a genuine love,
To chase a bat,
A spoiled brat.

A bird of a broad daylight
He bartered with
A pitch dark night's rat!

After it is too late
For a second chance
Towards his transformed lover
When he made advance,
Indifferent
She looked him askance.

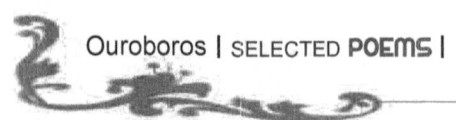

Soaring with wings of success

When we hand down
This flag to posterity
Paying prices of life
To the country's
Time-old sovereignty,
It is with
A word of caution
"This generation
Should accord
Due attention
To handing down
To the coming generation
A new Ethiopia
To fruits of development
A cornucopia!"

"Yes, grandpa
Working day and night

We shall take Ethiopia
To a new
Developmental height!

Once, Ethiopia was great
How could we that forget?

The country's renaissance
Firm we shall advance!

For common growth
Resources we
Shall harness,
Allowing the region
Soar with wings of success!"

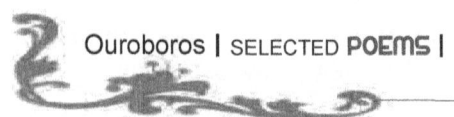

Soft Money

Deciding
To be kind
For those in need
I gave money off hand.

But soon
I turned cruel
When many took my giving
A for granted rule!

Savory,
Spoils many
Soft money!

Sorrowfully

"As you are bewitched
By my beauty
Allow me to be a bit naughty!
Pleasure expect not to gain
Without a little pain.

Take me to
The most expensive
Restaurant that does exist.

Let me order dishes top
On the menu list.
Hurry, let us go
To another place Having for
an open-kitchen
A space.
Don't you doubt
I have interest For a
non-stop bout.

Buy me

Expensive cosmetics

And shoes

Dresses and an overcoat

And what not?

Not forgetting

Money for transport.

Though

I was broke

When you got me first

I had a pride

Strong like a rock!"

Although you seem a dove,

A wolf in a sheep's skin,

You are blind

To a genuine love,

Hence, I have decided

The problem to solve!

Before you jilt me

When I have nothing
For you to siphon,
Finish with you
I ought
As love must not be
A typhoon!

So a fake dove
Helpless, may help you
God who is above.

Stood on its head

She made me a cuckold

With my best friend

"Go ahead

No problem!"

I said

And made love

With her close friend.

When life stood

On its head

"How dare you two?"

She said,

And in vain

Tried to trap me in bed

Planting a kiss on my forehead

"Darling the winner of

My bread."

"I am afraid

I have tasted the meaning of
Life to the full.
So don't be a fool
Be cool
And taste him
To the full," I said.

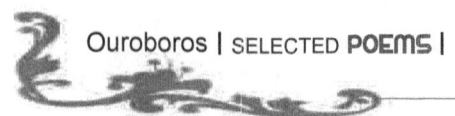
Stop licking a wound

Cute girl, a dove
You grew up expectant
Of an inviolable love.

But, know there are things
You should, such as
Unfold the unexpected could.

Cute girl, ingratiatingly
Enjoying a green light
To the citadel of
Your girlhood
At the height of your
Virginal beauty
Holding you close nude
Adept in creating
The required mood,
A fickle womanizer may
Suddenly leave

You for good!

Sister you should have
Seen through
Mr. Fickle's lack of personal
Integrity and internal beauty.

So cute girl, please brush aside
Your self-pity-packed song
"My love for Mr.Fickle, who adorned
with my chastity, is
matchless and strong! "

Also cute girl,
Know you should
Punishing Mr.Fiddle
For Mr.Fickle's mistake
Is the worst displacement
You could make.

Thus, cute girl
Better focus on the fact
You will be an efficacious cure
To a genuine lover yearning

For you with a heart pure!

The lovelorn
Mr.Fidel,probably
Injured by Miss.Fickle,
Terribly clamors for your help
To nurse him and
To get him back in shape.

The past you will
Cease to rewind
Soul and body
With lovelorn Mr.Fiddle
When you get entwined!

When pricked with a thorn
Barefooted farmers
Pull out the thorn
With a thorn
So cute girl pull out
The ungrateful Mr.Fickle
With the grateful Mr.Fiddle
That way the problem
You could settle!

Tardy in dawning on me

"Observing a man
Walloping his cat
For mewing without respite
Gripped by me-next fright
A dog kept quiet,
In a pitch-dark night
When a thief
Heading the gate past
Stole into a hut!"

Read this tale to me my aunt
When I was
On the wrong side of an infant,
To hit home,
"Never bury the fact!"

With a dump eye
I condoned the demotion
Of colleagues

Who asked
"Injustice and ill-treat why?"

Anon,my turn turned up
And I suffered a deadly slap!

Bubbling up from my memories back
The meaning of the tale
I heard four decades back
Appeared to me stark
When I suffered
A similar baseless
Power-exercising attack!

Teacher

With an insatiable urge
For your walk
Chalk and Talk
You illumine the dark
With eternal spark.

Teacher, you torch bearer
You render meaning
To the gist of living
Burning and shining
A lighting candle
Every passing second
That does dwindle.

For posterity you pave way
Which is your sole pay!

Though poverty
Is attached
To your holy profession
Keep on building a nation!

Terrorism

"We have
A winning formula
To paradise,
'Don't you that realize!'
If opting out
To go to hell if you dare
Smart, we shall
Escort you there!"

The acid test of love's intensity

"Even for a fraction of
A second
You,I don't want
To miss!
In dancing attendance
On you
I will never be remiss! "
This was your pledge
When in an eye-opener
Romance we were on
The same page.

Also it was your
Wont uttering
"Allow me please,
Now and then,
On your dainty lips
To plant a kiss! "

Putting at risk
My health
Passing through
The valley of death
I gave you an offspring
Which we found
A miraculous
And strange thing!

When fantasies
To responsibility
Ceded place
You made a habit
Driving me
To the end of
My patience!

You drop to a pub
For quick once
With your
Bachelor friends,
Who affectation-packed
Affection on you dance
To come home losing balance!

I don't think
You will lack
"Quick you have
To get back on track!"

Standing firm
And close by
A lactating spouse
In the teeth
Of responsibility
Also adversity
Is the acid test of
Love's intensity!

You must not
Jump ship
The cream of the cake
After you did sip!

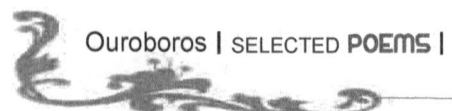

The bad boy mentality

Unless you prove
A bad boy
Many a girl could
Hurl you
A broken toy
Let alone
Your company to enjoy!
'Cause suspense-devoid
life
Predictable, is rife!'
Add to that
In declaring
The sentiment
You entertain towards
Your dream object
Be less fast
To avoid a love blackout.

The better evil

Intimidated by political thugs
Prone to insert in one's mouth
The nose of a loaded gun
Or suspend
A plastic bottle full of water
On males' reproductive organ,
Devoid of freedom of expression
Also denied the chance to his right
And deplorable condition
Drawing others' attention
Shunning his God-chosen land,
What is more
A bright and warm country
Under the sun,
A journalist dreaming began
Fighting all odds between
The deep blue see
And the angry Satan
To migrate to a better place,

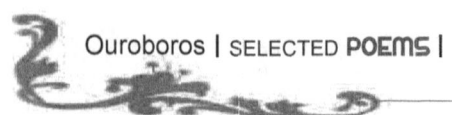

Where for democracy
Avowedly there is
A better space,
Inhabited by civilized people,
Averse to discrimination
Based on race!

Burning his boat,
Crossing desserts,
Crammed with other refugees,
Packed with him in a boat
Some trying to reverse
Their economic lot,
Surfing uncharted waters
Seeking a paradise on earth
He headed to
The country he sought
Though some their lives
At the hand of
Brutal traffickers lost
Beaten and thrown
Out of the boat,
Also at a port

Suspected of a terrorist bent
Many migrants
To prisons were sent.

After a humiliating acid test
Why for a dreamland
His country he left
As migrants' bane
They placed him at the foot
Of an ice-clad mountain.
"I will never see
My country again,
You are trying my patience
in vain! "
He vowed
Despite the razor-sharp
Cold untold.

Then,they took him up higher
An epitome to a cold fire!
Once more
He put his foot down
Putting on more clothes and
Changing attire.

They placed him
At the mountain's helm
As hell dark
Where the angel of death
Is seen stark.

Then in his head
Something began to bark
"You rather choose
The better evil
If both your assailants and hosts
Are mirror images of the devil! "

Seeing first hand
Those with cold shoulder
Refugees adore to attack
Though there are
Few not off humanity's track
At last he decided to return back
And under his country's sun bask
Mum for his rights to ask
Killing his journalists knack!

The clamor of the silence

After the burial of
A neighborhood child
I stayed in the cemetery
Where lush grasses, trees
And weeds grow wild.

Out of curiosity,
Inscriptions on
Headstones
I began to read.
At the height of
Her girlhood
To her parents' grief
A lass cut brief.

I noticed as runs
The adage
"Drinking one's cup

To the last dregs"
Few had passed away
At a ripe-old age,
Some had ceased to be
Of natural cause
While others
From the challenges
Life is sure to pose.

Reading, I went deep
Into the quiet wood
As far as I could.

A pregnant woman
Hit by a car
A man shot dead
In a bar!

The clamor of
The silence
Nudged me
While I still have
The license,
Repentant,my sins
I have to confess.

Then I heard
From right and left
"Had we been in your feet
We wouldn't waste a minute!
Your sins get rid of it
Do it!
Wash it!
Before God
You have to stand neat! "

"While in full harness
Sins ablution
Is what must come
To your attention!
Don't wait for
Days of retribution! "

Outside, I began my wits
To gather
To make an open breast of
My sins to
My confessing father!

The curse of the blessed

It is unfair
A barber's son should
Go with matted hair!

How come Ethiopia,
Africa's water tower,
Suffer for its crops
A timely reviving shower!

The double-faced

One can use

A knife to chop

A potato or a tomato.

Also getting off track

On can use it

To stab people

In the back!

Nations can harness

Nuclear to generate power.

To eliminate all

Or to tear down many

A tower.

The double-faced

Supper powers

That uphold imperialism

To meet their ends

Subtly cultivate

And promote terrorism.

They condemn it
Only if it wrecks
Havoc they
Don't permit!

Using terrorism
A midwife to a new religion
Or an independent nation
Even a false flag to meet one's end
From all quarters must be
Denied support and attention!

The flouted health

Wondering our dream
Comes true when
Every muscle we strain
Also unturned
We leave no stone
Pursuant of fortune.

But oft when
We strike fortune
Health the flouted wealth,
Bids farewell
Never to return again
Leaving a keepsake chagrin.

The gear changer

Running out of
Oxygen, burning out
When contenders feel like
Dropping dead,
In an unexampled manner
Summoning a vestige
Of energy
Bringing into play
A new strategy,
Miruts Yifter, Ethiopia's
Olympic legend,
Used to surge ahead
Demonstrating a race
Is a sport of foot,lung
And head.
That is why
A commentator
Christened him
"Mirutse Yifter
The gear changer!

The gear shiftier!"
"I dare say
Catching up with him
In a dead heat
There is no way
Once, he broke away!"

Two golds in 5 thousand
And 10 thousand meter race
In Moscow Olympic
With a gear-changing tactic
What a trick, what a trick!
What a story to children
And grandchildren to tell
Recalling minutest
Detail well!"

I recall
In our childhood,
With people
In the neighborhood
Our eyes to black-and-white
TV screens glued
We used to relish

Miruts' sprinted finish
Forcing rivals
Winning dreams
To relinquish!

After the medal
Putting on ceremony,
Heading to
Our football pitch
We used to run round,
Round,round and round
Till exhausted ourselves
We found!

It is adopting
Mirutse's footprint
Haile,Derartu, Kenenisa,
Tirunesh,Selershi
And Meseret sprint!
This formula grand
Gradually has found
Its way to Kenya
And England
May be tomorrow
To Sire lanka or America!

The great architect

Grinding and remolding a pot's shreds
A souvenir the master potter crafts.
So also from our pulverized pieces
A rosy prospect,God the great architect
Forth brings!

The great magician

I'm now sanguine
The ways of God
Are divine
Dream girl mine
Address that I fear
To endear
But who my very sight
Seems less eager to bear,
And the imbecile on me jeers
My pleas whenever she hears,
When months wrapped up into a year
In a campus confined near
As drips of water undoes a stone
My relenting love begin
Her heart to pry open.

Familiarity the great magician
Afforded me a ticket
Past her heart's gate.

The incident I never forget

To get a fresh air
A night stroll would be fair
I thought
And switching the TV
I got up from my chair.

On the pavement
Of a nearby apartment
A lovely girl by accident
I met,
Who looks timid and decent.
On my part a wink
On hers a response quick
Lovers soon we begin to click
And engaged in a kissing spree
On the street

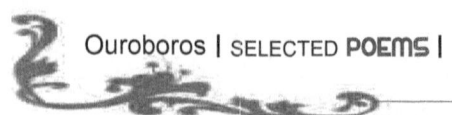

Our arms locked behind
Our waist
To passers by
Completely indifferent.

"My dear
Your lips
Are meant nonstop to kiss!"

"I was willing except
For time constraint.
You see home
I have to report!"

This way we were forced to part
Fixing an appointment.

Resulting in a great sorrow
It dawned on me on the morrow
She was a pickpocket
When I couldn't get
The wallet
I shoved into my back pocket.

From that day on wards
At night whenever I meet girls
And exchange greetings
I check my hands
For fear even
A finger could run amiss.

The independence tree

Like sands that ride a wind
Bullets all over strewed,
Dismembered limbs,
Soil mixed blood pools,
Bellies open ripped,
Visages smashed,
A decapitated head
On the forehead
A burrow that sustained,
A body half buried
Upside down turned
In a land, shell blasted
One leg a shoe deprived,
Blazed trees,
Charcoal burnt Tanks,
Two criss-cross
Piled up bodies,

Are the scenes
That sedated in my mind
With fire seared,
Once sent to a front
To compile a
Journalistic report
After a counter blow
That devastate
Aggressors were dealt.

Then after
When I see our flag
Flap up hoisted
Horizontally emblazoned
Green, Yellow and Red
Me it does remind
The independence tree
For million-years on end
That sprouted
Fertilized with martyr's blood!
And our sovereignty
That triumphed
Patriots' bone palisade!

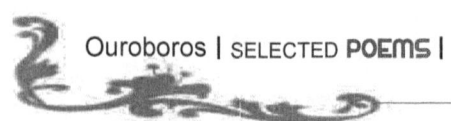
The last seconds

When a noose is lowered
Into a convict's head
In the last fraction of a second
Throng his mind
All sins and crimes he committed
He also regrets most
Why his crimes,in times good
He not atoned.
Also trails by his inward eye
From what he planned
But deferred to another day
And a greeting to his neighbors
He failed to convey,
Down to a small cloud
He sees in the azure sky
Elbowing its way
Sweltering under
The ferocious sun's ray!

The pitifulness of the pitiful

In a bustling open market
Before sunset
In buyers
And sellers heart
Seeking a place
An emaciated old beggar
With a weather-worn face
Was pitifully collecting alms
Putting on tattered clothes.

Soon in a tear-jerking
And heart-wrenching manner
A poor blind boy
Playing a flute
Singing a song strong
Titillating everyone's heart
Invoked sympathy with art
"It was
On a cursed morn

Blind, to a pauper family
I was born!
If given a stale
Bread to eat,
How could I
Despise it? "

With no need for
A second thought
Deducting from what
The hardest way he got
Touched, the old beggar
Gave the sight
Deprived boy
A Birr note
Though both were
On the same boat!

The pitiful have pity!
Is the lesson,
Among vendors and buyers
The incident drove home
Before draws nigh gloam!

The sky is the limit

A pitch dark night
Will be pierced by
A broad daylight
Seeds below the earth
That lie
Soon open eyes
To a heavenly father
In the sky
Then why?why?
Should you and I
Allow our ambition
Wilt and die,
See our dreams fly by
When say
A hurdle
Blocks our way!
We must never admit
When a dead end
We meet

There is no
Getting round it
We should know
When God shuts the door
He will open the window!

Hard we have to fight
To hit a target heartfelt.
The sky is the limit
Let us go for it.

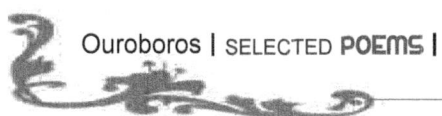
The sound track of life

Yes indeed
"Music is life's
Sound Track!"
As on the rail of time
An old song verse
Transports us back
A decade or a score
Even more,
To recollect
A quality time
With a lover
We spent
Though probably
Now the boat
Is irretrievably lost.

Or it makes us remember
How with a life partner

We vowed to stick together.

May be it mirrors
The grief
When our close person
Turned brief.

What is more
The things we did marvel
When on a travel.

Also it could conjure up
In our head
A historic watershade
To a new trend
That allowed a go ahead.

The survival of the slickest

The corrupt proving
To the development's wheel a spoke
Ironically changed the saying
"Walk your talk to talk your walk!
With "Cloak your walk
Behind your make-believe talk!"
Because it is a time for
"The survival of the slickest
Not the fittest!"

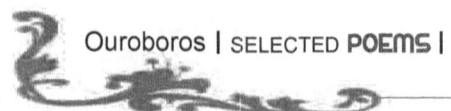
The value of silence

For keeping quiet
A body
Drives home fright!

The way of the dinosaur

You implored me
"My dove
Bestow your love
On me in bounty
As I am bewitched
By your beauty!"

Thirsty of my love
You terribly sought it a slave.

You vowed "Together firm
We shall see all seasons
Gadding to earth's ends!"
Pandering to my whims and fancies
You curried favorable responses
Adhering to your promises
Two lovely sons
With a four year gap

We brought up.
But nowadays remiss
To your commitments
After girls you hanker why?
Sexual arrears to defray!

My dear to obviate a fracas
Or before our home collapse
While I keep mum
Playing patience,
Curb your fantasies
For fledgling roses
Sick, I am effete of yours.

Unless one
Incessantly fans love,
Marriage's ember,
A marriage dubbed a hit
Could go the way of
The dinosaur!

They cross
fertilize

Peace and development,lung and heart
Feed on each other!
Preparing for war is option better
Adversaries to parry and deter.
Adverseries that conspire
The couple — peace &development —
to put asunder.

Also,to ensure peace,paying sacrifices further
Let us our development spur!
Unless they see
Poverty committed to the ground
And in their life a turnaround,
Daunted, to belligerence
Human beings are bound.

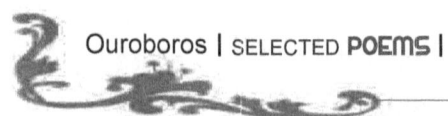
Time

Unilateral is your movement
Gliding fast away from the past
Neck to neck with the present
And moving deft the future to annihilate
And to the limbo of history to relegate
"The bygone days"or history of the past.

Knowing full well in gold
You are worth your weight
You are busy even for a moment
Your time to waste.

To hell I am inured

It was in
A backwater of development
Her childhood she spent
Where harmful practices
Mainly the fair sex that
Subject thrived rampant.

A blow on the row dealt,
Crushed, she sobbed and wept
Irritate at a community
Social filths that tolerate.

On her way to school
Raped by a woody pool,
She and her dream
For a life better
Got asunder,
Not to mention
The lacerating physical pain
She was forced to suffer!

A mental serenity deprived
Panicky rendered
Worse still
A sinful by all shunned
Her psychological carapace
To panic ceded place!

Scoffed, out from school
She dropped.

With few
To understand her position
She felt it a terrible sin
To give a red card to the seed
That forced its way in.

However,unable to withstand
Repulsion to the conceived
Revolt took the upper-hand
As it is not hard to understand.

After the conceived
A cherub turned

Qualms of concise assailed
Afraid rape second
In fleeing to town
She sought salivation,
Expecting people
With a touch of civilization.

There to a couple with a child
A servant she turned
And some skills she acquired,
But seduced by the husband
By the wife upbraided and slapped
Half her chicken fed salary deducted
To compensate for a glass
She clumsily in haste smashed
Herself she found
Cadging for bread
And shelter in the neighborhood.
By a dealer advised
And lured by what she heard
Hand me downs attired
A brothel she joined

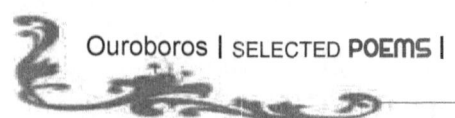
With feelings buyout
Inundated.
Nights wild she spent
With the fortune-and-alcohol run mad
Even the pilferers and the frustrated
To alcohol, 'Chat', sex-orgies
And hashish addicted.

So and so her health unheeded
She soon ailed from ailments
Of every kind
And took to bed.
To the God blest friends
Who brings her bread
This she said on her deathbed,
"As tradition bid
When my obituary is read
My body to my mother town ferried
And dust on me turned,
Make sure this is included
When before God I stand
And my case is heard
Where is your conceived?

And why my commandments
You haven't observed?
I will answer
It is the community that
Me born and raised
And cruelly molded bad shaped
Accountable should be held
For all I did ill-fate coerced
Besides, to hell I am inured
Thanks to 'you revering!' mankind.

So God
Hell if once more
I am to be remanded
Am I to be sacred?
From earthly hell
To heavily hell transferred!

To hide a bloodstained hand

"To hide a tree or wood
Plant it in a forest
One could! "
Practice that
Is what we should
To save our neck
When different courses
Time and history take.

Unless a circular we pass
For a handshake with us
How else and where else
Could we hide
Our blood-stained hand?

To win an argument
or remedy

Just to win an argument,
Oft, the couples
Resort to a heated debate.

For a change
They never tried
To remedy a challenge.

They have themselves to blame
For a solution-begging problem.

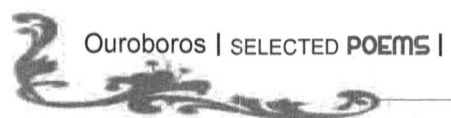

Trigger happy

In the vortex of
Passion wind
Sagacity down whirled
Trailing the drag
Trigger happy
I reveled.

With twisted arm
And broken bone
The hue from the passion
Out stroke and gone
Deposed from my throne
On a pile of mud
Ignominiously dumped on
I awakened anon.

Truth has more risk

"As telling lies
Is dangerous,
To it, you
Have to be averse! "

Parents, teachers
And society
Made me, cherish
This mentality.

Along the age road
The hardest way a new
Lesson I did upload.

Awaits those,
More risk
The truth
Who dare to speak!

For reporting strife,
Beating to
An inch of their life,
Or hacking them with a knife
Detaining the innocent
Has become rife.

Yet, come what may
Speaking the truth,
Is what I choose!

Unmatched grace

When a traditional
Music and dance,
Accentuating a century-old
Bilaterial ties,
Took place
A biracial and mesmeric
Greek goddess,
With chocolate Lucy's face,
Exhibiting elegance
With splendor
In my heart's citadel
Leased a place
Making it palpitate
Picking pace
Driving home
The intermingling of
This with that race
At times lends human beings
Unmatched grace!

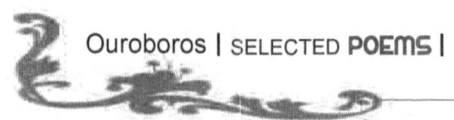

Use not a sword
for a word

True to
The saying
"The pen is mightier
Than a sword"
To your enemies
Deep-cutting and
Mask-divesting
Were every which of
Your acerbic and
Bitter-truth-packed word.
"An imminent danger
To ignore
His pen we ill afford
Nor could we
Fight him back
Word for word.
So covertly
Let us
Strike him down

With a sword
About his whereabouts
Effacing a word!" said
They, forgetting
As a writer you
Are worth your weight
In gold,
Whose books unprecedentedly
In large numbers sold.
Though some copies,
To gut down,
They did try to hold
Many were happy
To distribute
A hand-written copy.

Deep when you think,
Contemplating
Your pen when you pick
With it loud to speak,
Your subjects jump
Out of their skin
Scared of a basilisk!

Your pen
On your characters' neck
A pain
Was haunting their brain!
Yes your pen
Was their bane!

Dust to dust
You and also your enemies
With their swords
Had hopped on
Death's bandwagon
Yet your pen
Surfing the tide of time
Resurfaces again.

Vampires

With affectation
Kind-hearted and cool
Aid resources you pool
To dole it out with a spoon
And cream off
The lion's share
Of the boon!

I really wonder
What requital
Matches your sin
Of the vilest order!
What a conscience
That challenges you never,
To sustain life,
While thousands suffer
Disturbed by the knell
From the ominous sky
Roving vulture.

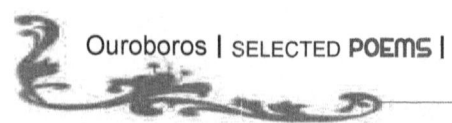
Welcome white dove

Welcome, welcome
White dove
You are an antidote
Border dispute to solve.

Welcome, welcome
White dove
Ethiopia's port problem
Eritrea's financial-return
Challenges
You are sure to dissolve.

Welcome, welcome
White dove
Tourism and trade
Must spur ahead.
So to wipe out
Dislike's filth
Let us put a glove.

Welcome, welcome

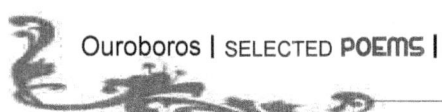
White dove
To make up for
Lost resources and chances
Also the two cousins
From dislike to absolve.

What a dialogue!

Life - >Death

" Why do
People see your
Behavior uncouth? "

Death- >Life

"It is simple
You are
A savory falsehood,
While I am
A bitter truth!"

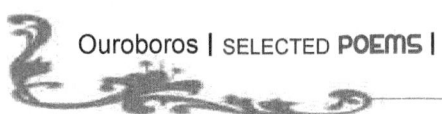

What a Fall

What a fall from grace
The untrustworthy are
Doomed to face!

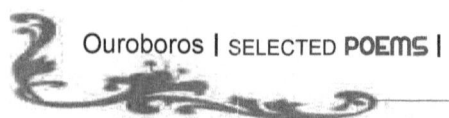

What a farce!

To polling stations
Going out in droves,
With their unanimous voice,
Electors made clear their choice-
"A breath of fresh air
Would be fair!"
But as a democracy patrons
Also democracy vendors,
You thought-
"Better an old satan
Than an angel new born,
The heart of a new angel,
We may not crack open!"

As peace brokers,
To dissuade voters
You dinned into their ears,
"Democracy is a process!
Thus it entails

The gradual unfolding of rights!
Specially in developing nations,
It is tardy in striking roots!"
You also went to say
"The ill-favored government,
Though by ballot card
Made out of play
And adamant to let power away,
A midwife to self-determination
Had paved the way
For the fairness you enjoy today.
Imagine the price it had to pay!"

Tirelessly you pleaded voters
To see reasons
And give the government
A time-out and stalemate,
Also to let it take part
In a joint government!
The hardest way
What people learnt today
Is democracy is indeed a process
That could suffer setbacks,

Or experience a lapse
And down clutters
A tyranny abyss!

Double dealers
Now as a democracy undertaker
You venture to offer
A hearse,
What a farce!

As history
Recorded it in its annals
Go ahead fish in troubled water,
By your very nature
You are incapable
To do better!

What a lesson

History has it that
"United we stand
Divided we fall!"
Was the secrete
That helped
The victorious
Stand tall.

Similarly A,b...Y and z
Ethnic groups all
Some major,while some
In number small
For ages were on the ball
Whenever there is a call,
Ever-ready nation's
Development spur
Or aggressors to deter.

Pursuant of a trick
"Divide and rule!
Fish in a troubled water
Putting siblings asunder"
The formula to the cruel
Tried z to dismatle A,b...Y's
Social fabric
Not sparing a single brick.

An upstart z drove a wedge
Among A,b...Y,on the sly.
But they asked "Dissension why?"
Isn't UNITY what in our
Formative years we bought!"
And together they went
For z's throat
To deprive it the devilish power
It terribly sought.

Now z is fighting a battle lost
What a lesson it got!

What a turn of fate!

While waiting
For a taxi
By a roadside
A young and
An energetic lad
Came and
Without courtesy
Pushed me aside
To take a ride
Hopping on
A minibus taxi,
Only for one
Occupant
A place had.

Before ebbs out
My vexation
Another taxi

Drew my attention.

I hopped in
Condemning a grave sin
The lad's action-
"Where is
His sense
of decorum,
Preached on
Religious and
Cultural forum? "

Fast, the second taxi
Almost caught up
With the first,
Which got out of sight
To be stopped
By a traffic light.

Out of sudden
I heard a deafening blast
That accompanied
Orange tongues of light

While the first taxi
Soared up like a kite.

With no need
To ask why
Such a thing
Happens out of
A clear blue sky,
Occupants and I
Out of our taxi
Managed to fly,
For we were
TV sensitized
To keep an open eye
Of terrorist that vowed
To operate on the sly.

Though sad
That cursed lad
Snatched death
From my hand!

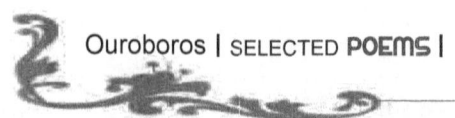
What a shift!

A girl friend

You used to relish
Proving my-fullfield wish!

A wife

You prove furious
And adamant
Unless you control
Every which of
My act!

What shall I be?

In a way that
Makes observers sick,
Shall I uncunningly
Side the slick?

Shall I optimize my chance
Echoing both
The good or wrong stance
Of who by unfair means
Seized the rein of power
And hence benefits
Will not be loath
On me to shower?

A chameleon,
Reflecting my surrounding
Shall I be
Self serving
As it has become
Nowadays a common thing?

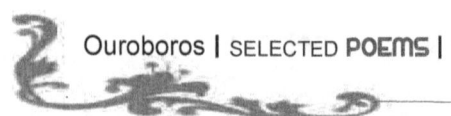

Shall I be an ermine?

Keeping my professional
And self integrity
And cleanliness
True to my conscience
To the extent of
Facing an unfolding adverse
Shall I distance
My self
From being
A false witness
On my colleagues
And neighbors?

What do I care?

Ravishingly beautiful
On top of that
God-fearing and cool!
What do I care
Electrified and petrified
Unable to resist her pull
At a loss how
My senses to pool
Up on catching her sight,
A wind-beaten leaf,
Shaking all over
I prove a fool?

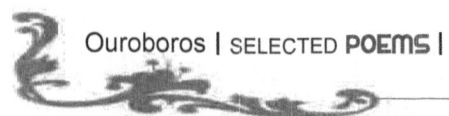
When peace is no longer under threat

For safely passing a pitch-dark evening
Under His protective wing,
Praise to the Almighty
Birds sing every morning
What a nice thing!

Whenever men broken pray
God's omnipresent ray
Their problem melts away!
Though unforgettable
Such a day,soon human-beings
Forget a prayer to say!

Why should men thanksgiving forget
When peace is no longer under a threat?

When will it begin to liquefy?

The sun with its
Fingers of ray
Caressing and dubbing
Thawed the ice,
Which a brook,
Soon bubbled
Forward to advance!

When will my
Lovelorn and
The frost of loneliness
Congealed soul
Begins to liquefy
In a way
Description that defy
Fine-tuned to
A soul mate's voice
And enticing eyes
With a heart
Engaged in ecstasy-
choreographed dance?

Which one is the saint?

Is it the pompous pope
That blessed off tanks
And hailed fighter jets
Bombs to drop,
On modestly armed patriots
Marching for a fair battle
Entertaining hope,
Not suspecting
A non-stop
Rain of
Banned-poisonous gas,
Lethal as Nazis'
Mass destructive soap?

What is more
Is it
The self-seeking pope

That sacrificed
An independent
Country, a push over,
Expecting a reward handsome
- an earthly kingdom?

Or

Is it the martyr monk
Who warned(cursed) the people
And the land
To Fascists
Not to give a hand?

What is more
Is it the
Selfless monk
By atavists atrociously
Gunned down
Scanning the sky for
A heavenly crown!

Who makes it speak?

Who makes water speak?

A rock!

Wipe Out your conceit

"God ,how could you find it
In your heart,
Me insensate to hurt?"

"How could you turn
Your face to my lot
Whilst a lot
From you I expect?"

"What is meant by
Out of a blue a bolt?"
" 'Who so ever gives a stone
To his child
Who asks for a bread?'
Is that not your word!"

God replied

"My son
Don't be a hypocrite
It is at one's low point
My mercy and power better felt!

It is my mercy
And benevolence alone
Tipping the balance
To one's weight
One in my eye's
Could elevate.
And always remember,
Praise should comprise
A major part of your prayer!
So wipe out your conceit
Kneel down and with
A heart immaculate
For what you need supplicate!"

With me forever it will stay

The very knowledge
That you exist
Affords me
A pleasure that has no limit!

Though the tide of life
Had taken you adrift
Between us creating a rift
Though it had cruelly
Taken you away
My love for you
With me forever stay
The way you planted it
In my heart
The first day!

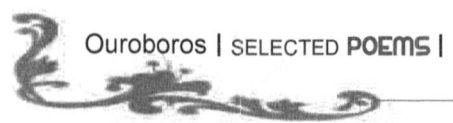

Yesterday,today
& tomorrow

Yesterday

A votary of democracy
And a combatant!

Today

A tyrant and a parasite!

Tomorrow

A prison inmate,
Who regrets
A wrong turn or bent!

You break anew to make!

A boy asked God
"Please give me patience?"

God to the boy
"I will send to you challenge!"

The boy to God

"I think we are not
On the same page
When I asked
You for patience
It was not for change!"

God to the boy
"Patience presupposes hassle,
In the remolding

Process to render you
Tolerant and gentle!"

Boy to God

"Yes hassle
To change
The peevish
To gentle,
I shouldn't forget
Your omniscience mantle!

You break
Anew to make!"

You have to pay for a deaf ear

Angry a man began to beat his dog
"Conniving with a thief is wrong!"
Answered the dog
"What more do you
Want me to do dear
After to my non-stop bark last night
You turned a deaf ear!

When told to mend its way
Adamant, the incumbent
Went astray.
After it is too late
It makes a dabble
To hold citizens to
The chaos accountable!

You too will be a victim

When you hear
Others back biting
Your friend
Listen assured, you too
On the morrow
Will be a victim to the trend!

Your coronation

For seconds closed shut
Organ senses mine the rest
Remained fettered my eyes
To yours, eyes that catches,
Sclerotic gems
From milky-stars hewn
At the cores
With jewels brown.

It is when
You looked me askance
With arched eyebrows
I realized at once
Though not
In so many words
I have declared
Your coronation
In my heart of hearts!

Youth

Lured by your
Elegant posture
When at its best
Appears nature,
Replete with optimism
Courage and adventure,
All welcome you
To lament and bemoan
Your quick departure!

Poetic dramas

<u>*A win-win approach (A poetic One-Scene drama)*</u>

Characters (All together six)
Ethiopia (Mother) , Blue Nile (Son) , Riparian
Countries (Two-R1, R2)
International Donors (Two- D1, D2)
A background music about Blue Nile River and a
backdrop about Blue Nile fall
(Abaye Negateba Habtun Yafesewal,
Chesalba Nedage Belew MenYansewal /
Day in and day out Abaye (BlueNile)
Pours down its wealth,
It will not be a hyperbole if
I dare call it the smokeless fuel)
The music slowly fades out
Enters Blue Nile (Monologue)

Unchecked and indifferent
I had been roaring past
Fast and vast

With a thunderous blast
When I fall from
A water mast.

The aura of my
Age-old invincibility
What is more
A prodigal river
My inviolable identity
Are stripped of me
By over 80 ethnic groups
That have begun
To display
Unprecedented unity.

So now
"Must I
My title defend
Or my wrong
Turns mend?"

*(Blue Nile kneels down
upon seeing his mother Ethiopia)*

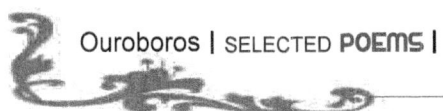

Enters Ethiopia

My repentant son
As the adages run
" 'United we stand divided
We fall! Also unity is strength'
You must understand
When siblings unite
To their mother's delight
They acquire power
Undauntedly challenges to fight
Conquering the unconquerable
To emerge triumphant.
Now fruits percolating
Across the board
Nation and Nationalities
And Peoples'
Bonds tightening
Every morning,
With "Unity-in-diversity-diversity" song
Emerging ever strong
They are displaying
A developmental leap frog"

Music
(Behere Behereseboche Nu Nu Yethiopia lejoche/
Come, Come Nation Nationalities
and Peoples of Ethiopia)
Ethiopia pulls up Blue Nile that is still kneeling

It is never too late
To start anew,
Blue Nile, my prodigal
But now repentant son
Contribute your due share
You can!

Your mother your nation
Deserves focal and
Undivided attention.

Blue Nile

Yes an imbecile or
An idiot
How could that
I forget?
A cooperative hand

To you I will lend
My indifference
To mend.

Yes democracy
When roots send
A nation
A self-development ladder
Could ascend!

Ethiopia

Forgetting differences petty
Whenever siblings
Both home and abroad
Portray unity
Their mother could
Expect bounty,
Whose benefit could
Accrue to
Neighbors true.

Blue Nile

Yes mother
If siblings have

Harmony and love inside,
By that is what
They abide
In their relation outside.
Continent-wise, marked
A peaceful nation
For peace keeping mission
Ethiopia is drawing attention.
Natural Sound Blue Nile falls

Enter riparian countries

R1 speaks
"If a
Win-win—hydro power—
Approach is what
You see fit
So be it!
Lose-win was what
Into your ear
We used to din!"
"Yes, Yes
Riparian countries,
We, can unite
Together to take

Our region
To new
Developmental height!"

R2 speaks

"Yes, yes for
Our industries
We can borrow power
From cooperative
And considerate Ethiopia
Africa's water tower!

Also lesson we did get
Mobilizing citizens
Behind development
To throw full weight."

Enter Donors (Two D1, D2)

D1 speaks

"Project proposal
We were oft prone
To reject.
Also finance
By no means

Without a string
We liked to inject.
Cognizant of this fact,
Galvanizing the mass
Bringing into play
A mega project
And handling
Daunting tasks
By oneself as
An object,
A project-financing,
Unexampled push,
Ethiopia has set
The finance constrained
To emulate."

D2 speaks

"Indeed, Ethiopia
Deserves high five
For its
Developmental drive!"

(Music Ethiopia national anthem)

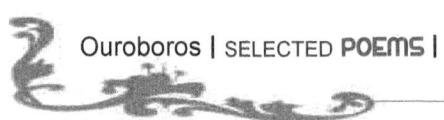
A Poetic One Scene Drama

Forward looking let us capitalize on the good deeds

Legacies
Introduction before the curtain is opened. The
introducer addresses the audience

Instead of none-stop
Condemning the past
Let us do our part
To lift our country From
economic morass fast.
Better than licking a wound Taking
corrective measures
On former leaders' mistakes
We could
Capitalize,on what they did good.

(Open Curtain) Enters Emperor
Twederos II

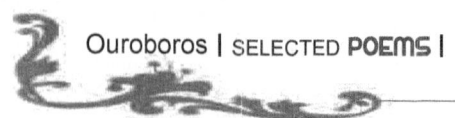

I had tried
Citizens to unite
So that
They will not
Stop short of might
When invaders they fight!

I had also exemplified
Portraying a spectacular
Self dignity and pride
Whatever sacrifices
Trying times demand,
A coward,
An Ethiopian must not
Yield a hand.

To convey
I had also tried
Though possible
As a tourist,explorer and
Even a covert spy
To enjoy one self in

Ethiopia, famed for
A hospitable land,
The impossibility
To carry away with
A shoe
Ethiopia's golden
Silt or a sand.

Enters Emperor Yohanes IV

In the battle of Gundat
And Gura
I had shuttered
Egyptians Khedivi's
Their advisers Europian
And North Americans aura.

Revolted by
A scramble for domestic power
Or salivating for wealth
And abhorring
Stooping to things glittering,
Defending my country

And faith
Valorous on the forefront
Of a battle
I did shake hands
With the angel of death.

Successors,
There are lessons
You should learn
Adoring your country
Rent seeking
You have to shun
Putting my country first
A notable self sacrifice
As I had done!

Enters Emperor Menelik II

Simply with
A sword and a spear
Carrying a shield
And riding a horse,
I did chase out

To its teeth
With modern weapon
Armed invading force.

When citizens
Join force and unite
With golden ink
History they can write
History that flickers light
The oppressed,worldwide,
Could win if they fight
For their
God-bestowed right.

Also to modernization
According focal attention
Must be the task of
A given nation
If ignorance and disease
Their tight grip
Must cease.

Enters Emperor Haileselassie I

When many warned me
"Do not forget
Your good gesture
You will live to regret!"
To the development of
My country giving
Focal attention
I allowed students pursue
Further education.
I allowed many to learn
And their poor country,
Serve in their turn.

A prophet
I exposed League of Nation's
Double standard
So that
The world underssstand
"Though today
Ethiopia's turn
The flame of Facizim
And Nazizim
Tomorrow

Supper powers too will burn!"
It was my wont
In the diplomatic mission
To bring
My country to the front!

Along with fellow leaders
It was my dream object
To de-colonize
And unite the continent.

That is why many
Saw for a continental seat
—OAU later AU—
Ethiopia fit.

President Mengistu

As revolution
Was the day's talk
With the progressive
I broke
On peasants and
The proletariat

Imposed yoke.
Said Barre's
Unexpected attack
And intrusion
I had managed
To reverse back,
Also fighting
Mass illiteracy
Was my
Outstanding task.
I did try to keep in fact
My country intact.

Prime Minister Meles

Ensuring freedom,
Political pluralism
And democracy's advent
Was my life-long
Cherished bent.
For this lofty cause
Selfless, my youth and
Adulthood I had spent.

Undaunted and brave
I and combatants
After tyranny
Sent to a grave
We invited soon
Marginalized states
To come aboard
And equally enjoy
Development's boon.
Innumerable farmers
Who rose to hero
From zero,
Many a woman
Who enjoyed a chance
To demonstrate
Their acumen
And also
The youth
Who shot up
From rags to riches
Confirm this truth.
Today a school,

A health station
Is not hard to find
In every nook and cranny
Of this from a dark past emerging
Out nation,
Over two decades back
Where delivering mothers
For want of roads
And infants lacking
Proper treatments die
In vain clamoring "Why? Why?"

I had also brought
To the global
Peacekeeping limelight
Ethiopian soliders
Well trained, valorous,
Efficient and polite
That mollify
Others' plight.
In the diplomatice front
In the fight to shift
OAU's seat

Conversant and in
Dramatically lightning-quick wit
Conspirators I managed
To defeat
In a manner such
A folly they will
Never think to repeat.

In an astounding
Developmental feat
I was out
The unconquerable
—Blue Nile—
To beat.

Also against poverty
A similar victory repeat.
What is more
On the road
Of Renaissance
I did inspire
Over 80 ethnic groups
Forward to run
Actualizing a leap in

Their life span.
A win-win
Environment smart growth
Was what,charismatic,
On the global arena
I brought forth,
Making super powers believe
Giving attention to Africa
Is worth.

Prime Minister Hailemariam Desalegn

In trying times
Not to allow
Started mega projects
Suffer a setback
I saw to
Things are on the right track.

More than one cabinet reshuffle
In the leading party
Deep renewal and reform,
Together with members,
I did perform!

To peaceful power transition
I have set a glaring example
A move

In Africa many took unthinkable!
A verse to rent seeking
I am patted on the back
"You have done a nice thing!"

Close Curtain
Introducer

Conspiracy
To grab the rein
Of power
At the cost of harm
Allowing one ethnic group
On others to tower,
Sluggishness in resource
Utilization, not allowing
Development to equally
And fast flower,
Harboring fright
When citizens exercise
Their democratic right
Are follies
The coming generations
Have to fight
So that
Ensues peace
And days bright.

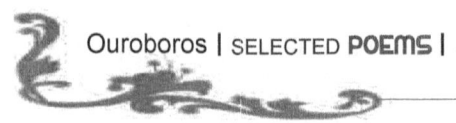

Feedback

//Blog poemhunter.com/Poem: What Shall I Be? / By: Roseann Shawiak/ Comment: You have an amazing ability to state underlying facts about important issues and human foibles. I really enjoy reading your poetry, Alem! Your imagery is solid and unmistakable, rhythm is usually very good, every once in a while it stalls, but for the most part is excellent. Thank you so much for sharing. //

//Blog poemhunter.com/Poem: Moral/By Jesus James Llorico/Comment: Short but true..rated 10+//

//Blog Poemhunter.com/Poem: When Will It Begin To Liquefy? /By:Mohammad Ahmadizadeh/ Comment: It sounds very pretty and lovely. I enjoyed reading it. Thanks for sharing your poem, dear poet.//

//Blog poemhunter.com/Poem: Love/ By Edward Kofin luis/Comment:Care to the beloved is ensured. Nice!/ Also By Khairul Ahsan/Comment: Read this poem of yours, it's very nice. Thanks for sharing your personal experience in the form of Poet's Notes. 'But it is the negative good' - Not sure of what you might have meant by this expression. Shall appreciate if you would explain a bit.

(Alem's explanation: Not optimizing one's benefit at the cost of harm to a lover.)//

//Blog poemhunter.com/Poem: - Youth/By: Anil Kumar Panda/Comment: It comes so late and goes away so soon. Wish I could get back my youth. Liked it.//

//Blog poemhunter.com/Poem: Youth/By: Akham Nilabirdhwaja/Comment: Youthfulness is so temporal that one laments at its quick departure. A nice poem.//

//Blog poemhunter.com/Poem: Opted To Escape/ By: Anil Kumar Panda/Comment: Short and to the point. Very nice.//

//Blog poemhunter.com/Poem: What A Fall?/By: Akham Nilabirdhwaja Singh/Comment: True, an inspiring poem. I liked it.//

//Blog poemhunter.com/Poem: Had I Not/By: Anil Kumar Panda/Comment: Very nice! Thanks for sharing.//

//Blog Poemhunter.com/Poem: Realizing His Kingdom/Member: Ratnakar Mandlik/Comment: The beginning of wisdom is realizing His kingdom.

The faithful are always rewarded by Him whereas the atheist, who question His very existence, have to face a lot. Thanks for sharing.10points.//

/ Blog Poemhunter.com/Poem: Fortunately It Resuscitates/By: Roseann Shawiak/Comment: Another excellent poem Alem! It is refreshing to read a poem about restoring nature and making it recover. It's a very admirable effort on the part of everyone in Ethiopia! You are all to be commended for doing this remarkable deed! In doing so you are also helping mankind and making life better for everyone there. Thank you for sharing this important information, I totally enjoyed reading about it. Thank you for sharing. //

//Blog poemhunter.com/Poem: What Shall I Be?/ By: Edward Kofi Louis /Comment: Reflecting my surrounding! Thanks for sharing this poem with us.//

//Blog poemhunter.com/Poem: A Linchpin That Doesn't Fit The Axle!/By: Kelly Kurt/ Comment: An insightful and nicely penned piece, Alem//

//Blog poemhunter.com/Poem: A Hell Turned Paradise/By: Amelia Cavazos/Comment: It is written nicely, and I love the meaning behind the words. Turning something so heart wrenching into something so equally heart wrenching, it isn't easy. Beautiful work.//

//Blog poemhunter.com/Poem: You Too Will Be A Victim/By: Edward Kofi Louis./Comment: With the muse of the negative acts of mankind on earth today. Thanks for sharing this poem with us.//

//Blog poemhunter.com/Poem: Bouncing Back/By: Edward Kofi Louis/Comment: Rejection! But, hope lies ahead. Nice work.//

//Blog poemhunter.com/Poem: Bouncing Back/ Member: Shakil Ahmed/Comment: Lovely poem with lovely thought, you have composed the poem very well, thanks for sharing.//

//Blog poemhunter.com/Poem: The Wise And The Fool/ By Member: Liza Sudina Comment: Tired of fools in my life. Nice poem!//

///Blog poemhunter.com /Poem: A Shock Treatment/ By: Roseann Shawiak/Comment: Excellent poem Alem! Yes, we must watch what we pray for,being human we sometimes forget the important things like our health in our quest for riches. Very well written with great meaning for everyone. Thank you for sharing.//

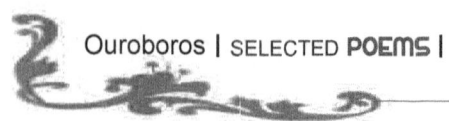

//Blog poemhunter.com/Poem: The Incident I Never Forget. By: Kinyua Karanja/Comment: Some say when the deal is too good think twice, some use their innocent face. I like it.//

//Blog poemhunter.com /Poem: No Condom No Sex/ Member: Roseann Shawiak/Comment: Interesting concept on an age-old problem, showing both sides of the situation, attempting to paint a complete picture for everyone to understand. Man's nature may be unpredictable, but so too is a woman's. Yet all do have self-control and need to exercise it, instead of giving in and ruining the lives of people they claim to love. Very good message contained herein. Thank you for sharing.//

//Blog poemhunter.com/Poem: To Win An Argument Or Remedy?/ By: Roseann Shawiak Comment: So true the words you have written, why do people think that getting angry will make their argument any better than the one they're arguing with. Yelling and trying to talk over another does nothing either, for they will tune you out, making you waste your breath. Why haven't they figured out yet a solution for what they disagree on? Don't let the sun set on your anger is how I live, it makes life so much easier. Thank you for sharing. //

//Blog poemhunter.com/ Poem The Incident I Never Forget/By: Valsa George/Comment: Instant love can come to a stop instantly! Better be on one's guard! All that glitters is not gold! A lesson learnt in the hard way! Enjoyed this interesting narration!//

//Blog poemhunter.com /Poem : Attention To Its Grotesque Faces/By: Roseann Shawiak Comment: Yes, corruption does have many faces, and it seems our politicians have the ugliest faces! Stealing from the people to line their own coffers and causing rampant poverty throughout the country. We must all keep exposing the corruption and graft in our governments,along with voting them out of office, and studying every person running for office with a fine tooth comb. Beware of those who are devils in disguise, like Obama, who has tried to ruin the United States. Everyone must fight the destruction of their countries in order to save their people. Thank you for sharing.//

//Blog poemhunter.com /Poem: A Hell Turned Paradise/By: Roseann Shawiak /Comment: Your words are true, cheating by a partner is pure hell, deadlier than death, it rips your heart out and tears your soul. My heart goes out to your friend (a victim to a similar problem mentioned in poet's note), it is a difficult thing to have to deal with, there are so many other women out there who deserve a love that's true and would never cheat on them. Hopefully, one will find him soon. Thank you for expressing the pain of a cheater's lies, it may help others to know of this deceit that could happen to anyone.//

//Blog poemhunter.com /Poem: Dust/By: Aftab Alam Khursheed/Comment: A very powerful write- dust and to dust you shall return! Thank U.//

//Blog poemhunter.com /Poem:Have You Visited Your Brother In Need?/By: Aftab Alam Khursheed/ Comment: We all are bounded by relation... That is trees of single seed... what charity if can't tender when brother in need... your writing is very powerful giving a mental jerk to think. //

//Blog poemhunter.com /Poem: What Shall I Be?/By: Anil Kumar Panda/Comment: Absolute beauty. All humans are not equal. Have to respond after studying them. Nice.//

//Blog poemhunter.com /Poem: What Shall I Be?/ Member: Gajanan Mishra/Comment: Self-integrity and cleanliness- life.//

//Blog poemhunter.com /Poem: A true friend/By Chinedu Dike/Comment: An insightful portrayal of the essence of true friendship, elegantly brought forth with conviction. 'A friend in need is a friend indeed.' Thanks for sharing Alem//

//Blog poemhunter.com /Poem: The Clamour Of The Silence/By: Roseann Shawiak/Comment: Very sobering thoughts to ponder in a place where death has already taken place and there is no reprieve for anyone left there. While walking through, hearing your conscience telling you to repent before it's too late and you end up there too! Very profound thought process, Alem! Excellent poem! Thank you for sharing. //

//Blog poemhunter.com /Poem: A Tit for a Tat/ Member Chinedu Dike/ Comment:Beautiful and insightful. Thanks for sharing Alem./

//Blog poemhunter.com/ Poem To hell I am inured/ By Chinedu Dike/ Comment:An insightful narrative, elegantly brought forth in good diction with conviction. The trauma of rape is aptly captured in the piece. Thanks for sharing Alem,//

//Blog Poemhunter.com/Poem: What shall I be?/ Member Rose Kana/Comment Wao! Chameleons lack loyalty... good piece of art.//

//Blog Poemhunter.com /Poem :Divergent Paths/By Edward Kofi Lewis/It was with a kiss! Thanks for sharing this poem with us.//

//Blog Poemhunter.com /Poem :My princess/ Member Dward Kofi Lewis/You gave me children! Nice piece of work. //

//Blog poemhunter.com /Poem: Liberating the Mind Before the Land /Member Kelly Kurt/A powerful poem, Alem. The plight of these innocents has to be brought to the attention of every other person in the world.//

//Blog poemhunter.com /Poem: Love /Care to the beloved is ensured!/By Edward Kofi Lewis/ Comment: Nice work//

// Blog poemhunter.com /Poem What shall I be?/ By Edward Kofi Lewis/ Reflecting my surrounding! Thanks for sharing this poem with us. //

//Blog poemhunter.com/Poem: What Shall I Be?/ By: Yohanes Jemaneh/Comment: Wow! I like it. Back biting others is just mobs' behavior, while applauding when together.//

//Blog poemhunter.com/Poem: Must She Be Like A Fairy tale Princess?/By: Yohanes Jemaneh Comment: Wow, it is a wise decision to prefer the pious one! A good poem.//

//Blog poemhunter.com/Poem: Love Has A Timeless Appeal/By: Yohanes Comment: Yeah, love has nothing to do with barriers. It has its own flavor that never be forgotten! Thanks for this classic remembrance to the eternal feeling!//

Blog Writeoutloud (wol)/Poem: A Lake's Obituary/ By Colin Hills /Comment :Thanks for posting this poem Alem. It highlights a terrible situation allover the world but especially in poorer nations where the environment has come under such intense pressure from the activities of man. Madagascar is a case in point where there has been huge environmental damage. The UK-based charity Wildfowl and Wetlands Trust has been working to restore habitat and educate locals in sustainable fishing and farming practices in order to help save the incredibly rare Madagascan pochard which survives in just a few remote lakes in the north of the country. Our appetite for destruction makes me weep.//

//Blog wol/Poem: Come to Ethiopia/ By Member Harry O'neill/Comment: Alem,if they don`t make you minister for tourism after this one they`re not doing their duty.//

//Blog wol/Poem: Soft Money/ By Member M.C New Berry/Interesting and timely. There is the reality that need create a condition of giving which encourages a condition of need. And who exactly is the neediest – and to what purpose? The conundrum has no answer and can actually have a detrimental effect on those most willing to give - entreated at every turn in this modern world by the outstretched hand, singular and corporate. In consequence, the willing spirit becomes prey to a undeserved feeling of cruelty by NOT giving for whatever reason.//

// Blog wol/Poem: Ouroboros / By member Colin Hill/Comment: I think Ouroboros would have made an excellent title Alem - an interesting snapshot into the self-absorption of African politics - no doubt no different from ours here in the UK except maybe without the hired snipers to quell dissent. All the best. / By Cynthia Buell Thomas:Comment : You have made some strong, sure points. The metaphor is excellent. Actually, I think your given title is probably best, as the average reader probably doesn't know the term 'oroborous' at all. Excellent photo - very informative. /Comment to the comment by Alem Hailu Dear Colin Hill and Cynthia Buell Thomas thank you for the feedback. I created the poem as Colin said but on the second thought I chose Cynthia's remark mindful that readers may not know about Ouroboros !

Comment by: Harry O'Nehill. Never mind African politics Alem, Ouroboros would have made an excellent title of a poem about what this Brexit thing would be quite willing to do to the British economy.

With respect to Additional comment by Colin Hill, Cynthia, it seems I must be one of your 'average' readers as I had to Google 'Ouroboros' - either because I didn't know the meaning or I had forgotten or I wanted to learn more in order to understand the poem further. Whichever, I am curious to know how you define an 'average' reader? I have never presumed that anyone having taken the trouble to find a site like WoL and having an interest in poetry was in any way 'average'. (I've edited this paragraph as I felt my original wording was ambiguous).And as it requires some basic user knowledge of the internet - on which this poem has been posted - it seems unlikely that any reader happening upon this word in this context would not Google the meaning if desired. I sincerely do not have a problem with Alem's choice of title and it is interesting that he had considered using 'Ouroboros' in the first instant. Personally, I thought it was eye catching and intriguing although I am aware that 'Self Cannibalism' is equally so and in that respect I am in danger of eating my own tail!. But it seems we have a different view of our readership/Comment by Alem Hailu, Dear poets thank you for the comments. I am readying the collection of my poems for a print on -demand book,proofreading and page layout work. It is after I read your recommendations it dawned on me I can use both titles for my book as a title and subtitle together with the Ouroboros photo. Also what a nice blog www.writeoutloud.com is because I learn a lot every time,refine my skills and get acquainted to knowledgeable poets. Another poem of mine with a similar theme entitled 'Yesterday,today and tomorrow' is trending in Hello poetry blog. / Additional Comment by Collin Hills Good luck with the book Alem - I agree, WoL is a great platform for learning and improving one's writing skills. All the best, Colin//

// Blog wol/Poem: The Gear Changer/Comment by Raj Ferds/May his soul rest in pace. He will be remembered as a life changer!//

//Blog wol/Poem :A Maverick Seen Mentally Sick/ By Raypool/ Comment :I like the idea of writing like a parable with a deal of wisdom to inform and also entertain ! Thanks . /Comment to the comment/ by Alem Hailu/ "His poems are replete with yarns and he loves to tell one" was what my instructor of Literature Dr Akalu Getaneh once wrote a blurb for my book, A Vent to Stifled Emotions. Your remark is in the same wavelength. Thank you.
On www.allpoetry someone suggested the replacement of the second stanza by

"The thief unfastened
Four bolts of a tyre
The sales day
Got chastened
On owners sight
He ran away./

I want native readers' take on my poems!//

// Blog wol/By Mathe Jeffy/ Poem: A Maverick Seen Mentally Sick. "Really well put together. A proper story,with meaning too.//

//Blog wol/ Poem You Break Anew to Make/By M.C. NewBerry// comment: Very relevant in this old world of ours. Patience and understanding are of such importance in the human condition place them alongside tolerance and kindness...comprising the essential lubricants needed to oil the wheels of our ongoing existence together.//

// Blog Wol/Poem :Fresh 2 Decades Later/Comment by Harry O'Nehil/Alem, I like the clarity of the whole thing...and the humility in that third section. / Comment by Rose Caresely/Same goes for me Alem. Your best poem yet./Comment to the comments by Alem Thank you! It is nice to know there are good poemhunters and poetical friends who tell a good poem when they see one!//

/Blog Wol Poem: Breaking the Double Yoke/ Comment Harry O'Nehill/ Alem,I wish I could `come through` so understandably in a language that was not my own.//

//Blog wol/Poem: Divergent Paths/By Harry O'Nehill/Comment 1: Alem, This comparison between the Judaism in the person of the name Judah and Mary Magdalene is inventive in it`s use of modern English terms in a sacred story.Your `cross floor`, tight grip of the fallen`, hankered`,and particularly that ` Gave a red card to her cherished perfume` demonstrates that - even writing in a foreign language - you understand our colloquial meanings well. That last stanza certainly wraps the story up. (I don`t understand 30 Birr)

By Harry O'Nehill /Comment 2:Alem, Just `got` the thirty pieces of silver (forgive my misunderstanding, in that first paragraph, of the theme.) Mind your diction (though `un-churchy`- to English ears) is still metaphorically spot on about the Judas theme.

That `red card` (get off my field of play!) and `cross floor` (betray) and `heading to the path` (joining)... and `saved hard` (stressing the former effort). are good.Your use of the eponymous term Judah misled me. Comment to the comments by Alem Hailu/ Thank you very much for the insightful comments you give me and which I find very much helpful in honing my skills. In the dictionary it puts Juda and judah as similar. I think this needs some clarification. The tribe itself seems to have forgotten the crucified lover of mankind as the dishonest disciple. (Doing some research I have decided to use Judas of Iscarlot or Judas the Iscarlot in my book) //

//Blog wol /Poem: Liberating the Mind before the land. By Thomas Johonson /Comment : This has a great rhythm to it. Keep up the great work. There was a lot of emotion, and it invoked a lot of intentional imagery. I really enjoyed this./Comment to the comment by Alem Hailu/Yes you are right such feedback spur poets like me to fight injustice across the globe. You see lately I have joined a group, Poets Unite Worldwide!//

//Blog wol/Poem Love has a Timeless appeal/ By Lancashire Country Palatine Tourist Bard/ Comment: This is beautiful. It reminds me of the perfume of the wild roses which I always look forward to sniffing at, by the side of the country road where my wife and I frequently walk.//

Poem:Liberating the Mind before the land By Lancashire Country/Palatine Tourist Bard/Comment :Power to your Pen! Well said!//

// Blog wol/Poem: The Better Evil/By Tommy Carroll Comment: A harrowing piece Alem. It's awfulness came through after several readings. //

//Blog wol/Poem: A Shock Treatment/ By M.C Newberry/Comment The theme health is the real wealth is unassailable.//

//Blog wol/Poem: Think Before You Ink By M.C Berry Comment/A good point. Never commit to something impossible to remove or change—with the exception of love.//

// Blog wol/Poem: A Tit for a Tat/By Cynthina Buell Thomas /Comment: Strong message,strongly expressed. Excellent Opener to stimulate readers interest.//

//Blog wol:Poem : Devil Could Not Be God/ by Harry O'Neill/Comment: For someone not writing in his native language your poems are getting more poetically understandable every week.//

//Blog Wol/Poem : An Ape's Bald Butts/By Cynthia Buel Thomas/Very funny—Love the play on up. Spears a strong point too.//

//Blog Wol/Poem: The Clamor of the Silence/By Raypool/Comment: This very much appeal to me or it has a moving simplicity to it and reaches out in a personal sense, may be in the same way as someone who by luck been spared away catastrophe and sees and tells uncomfortable with the others who have passed away. Interesting concept.//

// Blog Wol/Poem: The Clamor of the Silence/ By M.C Newberry/Comment:Identify with the inspiration of these lines. Sometimes a successful search to locate the grave of my late father's 1ˢᵗ cousin murdered by Michel Collins's hit men on the original blood squad in the adjacent grave which told a tragic story when I put on my poem "A tomb stone tells a tale."Cemeteries have much to tell us much in fact to teach us if we take time.//

//Blog wol/Poem: Have You Visited Your Brother in Need?/ By Martin Elde /Comment : Very good Alem. It jogs along at a good pace. It is quite evocative. Welcome to Wol./ By Patricia and Stefan Wilde/ poem: Have you visited your brother in need. Comment:Welcome Alem. Extremely powerful writing!We really look forward to more of your outstanding work.//

//Blog Wol/Poem: A Far Cry From/By Patrica Rushe/True//

//Blog Wol/Poem : Different Sides of the Same coin/ By Harry O'Ne/Comment:A timely reminder that democracy can be liberalized too much.//

//Blog:allpoetry.com/Poem The Incident I Never

Forget: Comment By Harry O'Neill/It is her hands you must check.//

//Blog poetrypoems/Poem: With wings of success/ By angelsinthe mist /Comment :   Flows Nicely//

//Blog Poetry Poems/Poem: Preposterous/By Gesha Comment:Clever//

//Blog Poetry poems/Poem: Dust/By reflectivepoems/ Comment: Excellent!Ashes to Ashes Dust to Dust so says the big book//

//Blog   poetrypoems/On   the   Wrong   Heart/ roberthaigh/Excellent/Very Nicely expressed in just few words. Well penned.//

//Blog poetrypoems.com. Poem: Come to Ethiopia/ By Anglesin the mist. It is nice to read a poem promoting gratitude and unity. Thank you! By the grace of God all shall unite 4 peace in action & love in Flight---plant peace—2 show and grow love 4 heaven on earth---As stars aboveAdd a dash of humor humbleness too. 4 peace and love 2 really shine through.//

// Blog allpoetry/Poem :Different Attitudes of Mind/ By Sunnyde Majesty/Comment:Your diction is nice. You really hit the nail.//

//Blog allpoetry/Poem: Ravishingly Beautiful/By Melting Newtons/Comment: "Melancholy and fore lone at its finest. Clapping hands."//

//Blog allpoetry.com/Poem: A Maverick Seen Mentally Sick/By Walge Karren/Comment : I loved the story behind, to me was meaningful... to me lunatic asylums are the most clean places in the world just like monasteries. It is our assumptions what makes places to heaven or hell.//

//Blog allpoetry.com/Poem Fresh Two Decades Later/ By Judes Kiss/ Comment Nice Poem!Keep it up.//

//Blog allpoetry.com/Poem : Fidel/By Amancel 95/ "This guy understood righteous long before it's time. Some are born with natural gifts. How you proceed with it is another thing!"//

//Blog poetrypoems.com/Poem :A Far Cry FSrom./ By lijo 10/ In this season of Christmas I'm so glad I saw this. Like it. Just brightened up my day. Very well written. Poem on the joy...//

//Blog poetrypoems.com/Poem: Breaking the Double Yoke. By sno-flake/ I like this write!It was an interesting read."//

//Blog poetrypoems.com/allpoetry.com//Poem: Divergent paths/By Ronald Bullins/ This is a nice poem clever piece .I enjoyed reading this clever piece. Keep up the good work.//

//Blog allpoetry.com/Poem:Divergent Paths/By M.Atkins/Great share enjoyable.Traditionally it was Judas who betrayed Christ. However the house of Judah(from the 12 tribes of Israel)is where-if I am correct—the linage of the jewish people came through(as lots of the other tribes are scattered)

Anyways one could take your poem and the substitution of juda for judas-to be commenting on a belief—from a Christine view—the entire civilization betrayed Christ and Judas is just the scape-goat.//

//Blog allpoetry.com/Poem: Must She be Like a Fairy Tale Princess?/By Repent/Comment: Enjoyed it. It is lovely. That someone feel that way. May be I'm a bit cynical but this attitude to a woman(Or any person)surprised me.//

//Blog allpoetry.com/Poem: A Linchpin that Doesn't Fit the Axle./By Tamina J/"Keep writing. Great job on this,I thought it was well written."//

//Blog allpoetry.com/Poem: A toothless face/By SL123/Comment "Clever job. Cleverly written. Well done!"//

// Blog allpoetry.com/Poem: Mandela the Moral Giant/By Sherifmone /"Very recounting of a long struggle!"//

//Blog allpoetry.com/Poem :Mandela/ By Nana Kwane/Comment: Awesome. Mandela is one of my favorite good book, he wrote entitled Long Walk to Freedom speaking of apartheid very well sin. This plain abstract truth this world is misguided and you can make a huge impact on the way people think. Mandela will for ever live on.//

//Blog allpoetry.com/Poem :Love has a Timeless appeal/"True. I'm very glad you still hold love in such regard. I believe it is a beautiful thing and I hope to be such an example for someone one day. Beautifully brief piece."//

//Blog allpoetry.com/Poem: It Could Buy the Priceless Life./By Roger Turner/Comment:Lovely poem. Blood donation is one of the greatest gifts outside of organ donation one can give. At least with the first,you are not dead to do it. Well done.//

//Blog allpoetry.com/Poem : A Genuine Friend/By Bail Spire/Friends are awesome. Good write.//

//Blog allpoetry.com/Poem : Loss Amplifies the Merit of the Missed. By/ Very nicely done. Keep writing.//

//Blog poetrypoems/Poem: A Shock Treatment/By my poems 1053/Nice sentiment. I too wrestle with this dilemma.//

//Blog poetrypoems/Poem: No Condom No Sex/ By haley bissect/comment/Wow I have to read this again,love it already//

//Blog Hellopoetry/Poem :You Break Anew to Make/ By Tapiwa Individualist/

Why God allows suffering? Suffering was not part of the original plan .Because when man was created,he was already connected to God- the closeness that we now have to seek existed naturally. When man sinned, he had to start striving for a better life,a r/t with God, and also the search fort wisdom and knowledge. Suffering draws our hearts closer to God,when man sinned the original r/t was distorted therefore there has to be a way to draw us truly back to God,When there is suffering,there is deep humility that makes us surrender all to Christ b/c we acknowledge,that our strengths are just not enough. God wants us to love and trust him. Therefore, he is always with us through it all...

Sometimes we suffer because God is trying to remind us of his power and glory,to return to Him and not miss heaven. God loves you and he is very much alive.//

//Blog allpoetry/Poem: A better evil Chocebaldock39/ Great use of words really good. I would like to see you write more.//

//Blog allpoetry/Poem: Stop Licking a Wound./By Neuronimo/Well written. Liked your poem.//

//Blog allpoetry/Poem: Stop Licking a Wound./By Jolene C/No desire to punish him for anything. I simply want him to be happy.//

// Blog allpoetry.com/Poem: How to Tell a Fool?/By Angel Fizz: Cleaver reminder. Keep it up.//

//Blog allpoetry.com/Poem: A King Born/by Iman elsa Khawy/Great. What a wise father!Reminds me of king Lear but the last took the opposite direction.//

//Blog allpoetry.com/Poem: A Herd Mentality/By Rohn/Comment: Very well written—strong words for a strong subject. Keeping hold of tradition in an ever changing world is even hard in the West because we are a melting pot of diverse antecedents with to God- the closeness that we now have to seek existed naturally. When man sinned, he had to start striving for a better life, a r/t with God, and also the search for wisdom and knowledge. Suffering draws our hearts closer to God, when man sinned the original r/t was distrorted therefor there has to be a way to draw us truly back to God,when there is suffering,there is deep humility that makes us surrender all to Christ b/c we acknowledge,that our strengths are just not enough. God wants us to love and trust him. Therefore, he is always with us through it all...

Sometimes we suffer because God is trying to remind us of his power glory,to return to Him and not miss heaven. God loves you and he is very much alive.//

//Blog allpoetry.com/Poem: Inequality of All Shades/ By Katrina mcnaugher/Comment:I like what you have to say in this poem.//

//Blog allpoetry.com/Poem : Must your gratitude be a knife?/By K.N.C/Comment/Nice write. Very powerful message here!//

//Blog allpoetry/Poem :Must Your Gratitude be a Knife?/By Kevin/Comment:Happy to accept this into our book project, (Remembering Spring) thank you for joining us. It will be a lovely and unique addition.//

//Blog allpoetry.com/Poem :Is Capable to Mar/By The Fire Burns/Keep on it. Agreed.Well written.//

//Blog allpoetry.com/Poem: When Will it Begin to Liquefy?/By Tsunmai/Great imagery. The frost of loneliness congealed soul begins to liquefy. Learned some new words too.//

//Blog allpoetry.com/Poem : A Far Cry From/ By Muwanguzi./Comment:Great. I totally agree Christ is all about Christ not getting wasted .Great reminder.//

//Blog allpoetry.com:Poem: Remiss in Expanding/By ghosteyes/ Comment. Keep writing quaint flowing feels light and happy and flawless good write.//

//Blog allpoetry.com:Poem A True Friendship. By Raghavendran/Comment Inspiring. It is a fact that only true friends stick through tick and thin and the rest are fair-weather friends. They desert us when we badly need them. But that is the world.//

//Blog allpoetry.com/Poem: Double Victory/By Shanegalame/Nicely done .Interesting format.//

//Blog allpoetry.com/Poem : Diffrent Faces of the Same coin./By insanedemongirl/Comment/Enjoyed it. Good job. Liked it.//

//Blog allpoetry.com/Poem: Regretted I /By wisedrum/ Comment: Enjoyed it. A lesson to be learnt.//

//Blog allpoetry.com/Poem: The Sound Track of Life/ By Rghavndran Comment Liked it: Music is the nectar of the soul. It takes us back to time of intense happiness or to time of inexplicable sorrow. Except one who has no ears no one dislikes music of any kind. A good recollection of times through the music is what the poem talk about. A nice one.//

//Blog allpoetry/Poem A Stone Can't./By Babbling brooks/Comment:Clever piece./Nicely penned. I enjoyed this unusual piece. Thanks.//

//Blog allpoetry.com/Poem:Which One is the Saint/ By Riversong/Comment: Beautifully illustrated. Wonderfully written.//

//Blog allpoetry.com/Poem: A Shifting Goal Post/

By Lord james/Comment: Funny clever work.//

//Blog allpoetry/Poem: Devil Couldn't be God:By Worldsaway/Comment: Yes Satan would have been a good angel,but wanted too much,superb!//

//Blog allpoetry/Poem: The Pitifulness of the Pitiful/ ByNeelem7/Comment: Beautifully scripted. I enjoyed the style of your writing.//

//Blog allpoetry.com/Poem:What a Farce/By Livi Pearson/Comment Good.//

//Blog allpoetry.com/Poem: A Tit for a Tat/By Sweath Gupta/ Comment: Nicely done/My favorite line is Pot,Cry not foul,Nor must you bark,while it is stark you are a sooty reflection of a night,pitch-dark. I liked it.//

//Blog allpoetry.com/Poem :Newton 4th Law/By jim barruffi/Comment: Like it .Good one.My favorite line is lotion.//

//Blog allpoetry.com/Poem: Tight Rope/By Souju Mkishore/Comment: Liked it. All words great.//

//Blog allpoetry.com:Poem :The Incident I Never Forget/By Simplyjo/Comment: great poem//

//Blog allpoetry.com/Poem: Soft Money/By Random musing/Comment:Exactly, Mr.Alem in this fixed world today,even charity is not let free. Nice penning.//

//Blog allpoetry.com/Poem: Fire Balls/ By Lisa La Grange/Comment:I really like the metaphors you used to illustrate the effect of the girl. Great work.//

//Blog allpoetry.com/Poem: Fire Balls/By Senanrod9/ Comment: Excellent job. I love the use of the fire balls to describe her eyes. My favorite line is affixed on either side ...You really did a great job with this.//

//Blog allpoetry.com/Poem :Truth Has More Risk/ By shallbell/Comment Honestly Lovely. This is very fantastically and nicely written. The truth is a hard thing to come by. Nice job//

//Blog allpoetry.com Poem :A 180 Degree Turn/ By Jerome Riordan/I enjoyed this. There is a lot of them like that. I like lampooning politicians. Nicely penned.//

//Blog allpoetry.com/Poem: To hell I am Inured/By Taker Mccoy/Comment: Raped by a woody pool was horrifyingly direct,but true,I suppose, and that gives me a mixed feeling poetically. I feel the pain but not the poetry.//

//Blog allpoetry.com/Poem: Old Flame/By Queen enjoyably/Wow! Great post. Liked the line "Yesterday's old flame has conveyed to me the same!"//

// Blog allpoetry.com/Poem: Come to Ethiopia/By Tyna D.S/Excellent job//

//Blog allpoetry.com/Poem:Out of Bed Four/By Elias Fares/Great writing. Wish there were more. But this way every one can fill his own story.//

//Blog allpoetry.com/Poem: Revamped/B.sutah / Comment:I love it. I had it briefly so your words are bitter sweet. I thank you for waking some of my sleeping happy memories.//

//Blog allpoetry.com/Poem: Terrorism/By eyeeye/ Comment/Love it. Witty and lovely little poem. No need for more or less. Nicely penned.//

//Blog allpoetry.com/Poem: Quite Strange/ Comment:By spokeninsilence. Great write. Short,quick,sweet,paints a larger picture! Wonderful write,short but you get your message across. Keep writing I would like to read more of your work in the near future.//

//Blog allpoetry.com/Quite Strange/By Geetanjali Saini/Very enjoyable. Title apt. Something to work on is nothing at all .It is all quite cute. Like the way it goes sweet and easy breezed .Nice job.//

//Blog allpoetry.com/ Poem :Don't be a Sheep in a Goat's Age/By Frair/Comment: Greetings from Russia. Excellent work. My favorite line is an Ethiopian will never ever change his skin,take note nor could a sheep be a goat. Russians also say who keeps company with the wolf will learn how to howl.//

//Blog allpoetry/Poem: Your Coronation/Katerine 345/ Comment:Enjoyed reading. My favourite line Your coronation in my heart of hearts.//

//Blog allpoetry.com/Poem: When Peace is No Longer Under Threat/Comment: Soothing and it calls the reader to have a brief look at the content. The problem melts away. Very hopeful write. I will say. I like it//

//Blog allpoetry.com/Poem Soaring with Wings of Success/By erekrose/Comment: Title relevant. Favourite line is 'Yes grand pa working day and night we shall take Ethiopia to a new height.'//

//Blog allpoetry.com/Poem:The Survival of the Slickest/By fugitive/Great title. Favorite line 'Cloak your walk' So many do this. Keep writing.//

//Blog allpoetry.com/Poem: A Balm/by momsgirl2/ Short and gets right to the point. Being single is not something to dread. We all are alone at times.//

//Blog allpoetry.com/Poem :A Painful Satisfaction/ By anglekiss/A poet's dream came through. As one can see here, it takes time and effort, but the result is worth the pain!//

//Blog allpoetry.com/By Amenda/A Painful Satisfaction/ Comment: Intro wow it is great .My favorite line "At night When all is quite till I hit the nail right on the head I will never repair to bed."

//Blog allpoetry.com/Poem :Teacher/By Gene 86/ Comment:Loved it. Nothing I could nitpick at. My favorite line is"Which is your sole pay. I find these extremely true. Teachers despite having horrendously tedious and important job, are severely underpaid. I love how the writer tied this sentiment into the piece by associating the low pay grade with posterity and duty. I think this is a marvelous piece and very much deserving a praise. Teachers are very ,very hard workers and deserve far more credit than they get. I hope that somebody,every teacher I ever admired and loved will read this piece and become inspired to keep on,while knowing that there are indeed those of us who appreciate all they do. This is a wonderful work of Art and I love it.//

//Blog allpoetry.com/ Poem: Teacher By dead but moving/Comment:Inspired me. My favorite linen'For posterity you pave way. Which is your sole pay!True poverty is attached to the holy profession keep on building a nation.//

//Blog Allpoetry/Poem: The Survival of the Slickest/ By DMTz/Comment:True.//

//Blog allpoetry.com/Poem: Love/By Addietive/ Comment:I enjoy this. Favorite line is "By fair means or foul meeting ones end,but it is the negative good care to the beloved ensured. "This is a great poem.//

//Blog allpoetry/Poem Love/By Linda Pendent/ Comment:Short and sweet. It is sad so many people don't have this idea of what love should be.//

//Blog allpoetry/Poem: Have You Visited Your Brother in Need?/ Comment:Nice Job. Favorite

Line/'It is my brother in need?'//

//Blog allpoetry.com/Poem:Great Tiding/ By Asper/ Comment: Beautifully written/Favorite line 'But know you have extra work.'//

//Blog allpoetry.com/Poem :An Honest Despot/By Down in Holda/Comment: Clever work.//

//Blog allpoetry.com/Poem Think Before You Ink/ By Poet Shalkan/ Comment

I like this a lot. I worked in a tattoo shop & most of the cover ups we did were over ex-lovers names!Now you have options though. Cover ups with something you can be proud of,leaser removal, there is even a couple never techniques that involve removing ink with a tattoo making that work really well too!Good message though. I spent a lot of time trying to train couples out of the idea. It is hard though,when they are blinded by love.//

//Blog   allpoetry.com/Poem: Fortunately   it Resuscitates./By Travis Allen/ Comment :Lovely. Truly believes in that.//

//Blog allpoetry.com/The Clamor of the Silence/ By Declan Molloy/Nicely penned. Interesting piece. I

suppose Graveyards are good places for inspiration
.Nicely done.//

//Blog allpoetry.com/Poem :A Broken Heart Suffice/
By Jake the poet/Comment:Clever work. Your poem
brings to light how the creator can see through all
the bullshits. Such is the kindness,power mercy and
truthfulness of the king of kings.//

//Blog allpoetry.com/Poem :A Hell Turned Paradise/
By Indian/Comment:Enjoyed it. Great imagery and
metaphor. Nicely flowing poem too. Thanks for
sharing.//

//Blog allpoetry.com/Poem: I can't help to ask/This
is nice...Good work. Keep on!//

//Blog allpoetry.com/Poem :The wise and the fool/By
Daisy Bronx/Amazing. I love it. Simply powerful.//

//Blog allpoetry.com/Poem;An Overriding National
Feeling/By Mshram/Comment:It reminds the unity
of the world. I like the stanzas at the end started with
'It is b/c"This is awesome image of regional heritage
community and pride shines through.//

//Blog allpoetry.com/Poem: To hide a blood stained
hand ./ Comment:You liquid emotion. You actually

inspired me to write a very emotional poem with this.//

//Blog   allpoetry/Poem:What   shall   I   Be?/by shaddows/Good basspoem. Like it Good.//

//Blog Hellopoetry/Poem : A black empress's legacy(Tayetu   Betul)/By   Fasika   Berehane/ Comment::

Wow! Empress Taitu couldn't be expressed in much better way than this. Thank you Alem. It is so inspiring and a history to always feel gratified. Much respect to your works!//

//Blog wol/Poem A Black Empress's Legacy/By Cynthia Buell Thomas/Comment:Much appreciated and enjoyed it.//

//Blog/ www.allpoetry.com/ Poem: Stood on its Head/ By Charlotte C/Comment Stood on its head/ I enjoyed this read! Well done!//

//Blog/allpoetry.com/Poem: Cure a Wound Another Could /By Sanesanne/Comment: I really like this poem .Nice word choices, it really hits me.//

//Blog/allpoetry.com/Don't use a sword for a word/ By infinity111/Comment very revealing words about the power of pen and the tyranny of censorship as it may be all around the world or next door. Good luck with all your writing on here.//

//Blog poetrypoems.com(PP)/Poem: Liberating the mind before the land/By dandy1/Comment :Excellent The inhumanities man does and blame it on religion and God's will. In the end Heaven is crowded and waits only for the deserving few who can answer to their deeds despite Satans lies.//

//Blog PP/Poem: Like a Cigarette/ I can't help to ask/ A shock treatment/By Poet11586 Comment: Excellent. I enjoyed reading your poems. They are very well penned. //

//Blog pp/Poem : A Shock Treatment/ By mypoem1053/By Poet11586/ Comment Average/ Nice sentiment. I too wrestle with this dilemma.//

//Blog PP/Poem On the Wrong Heart/By Robert Haigh./Comment Excellent/Very nicely expressed in just a few words. Well penned.//

//Allpoetry/Poem A win-win approach /A poetic drama/By Klinton Helms. Comment:Amazing. Thank you for sharing!I could feel to a degree how you do about this. I feel inspired to learn more.//

//Blog/poemhunter.com/poem: Don't use as word for a word/By Rosean Shawik/ comment/Very impressive writing Alem!/ you have an excellent handle on English, your imaginary is very vivid and enticing.//

//Blog/Allpoetry /Poem:With me forever it will stay/ By Poetchil/Comment.You are a very good poet and you can pull a lot of chicks with what you write…Do a show!…Too.Keep on it too.//

//Blog/poemhunter.com/poem/Cure A Wound Another could/By Roseann Shawik comment: Excellent poem. I like how it is written.//

//Blog/allpoetry/Poem: The Pitiful of the Pitiful/ Comment by Neelan: A beautifully scripted poem. I enjoy the style of your writing.//

//Blog:allpoetry/Poem: An Ape's Bald Butts. By Foxx/Comment: Good job .Great one…Fun. Really,kool. No need for brevity.//

//Blog:alpoetry/Poem On the Wrong Heart/By tdc/ Comment: Lovely.So true an amazing post.Sir, a beautiful saying.//

//Blog:allpoetry:Poem: I Can't Help Asking:By

Xavier Liabunya.Comment.This is nice…Good work. Amazing. I loved it.//

//Blog allpoetry/Poem:What shall I be?/By Shadows:Good bass poem. Like it good.//

//Blog:allpoetry/Poem/Lovely/By Travishlyall:Comment:True//

//By allpoetry/poem: The clamor of the Silence/ By Riversong/Comment:Nicely penned.Interesting piece.I suppose graveyards are good places for inspiration-nicely done.//

//By allpoetry/Poem:Which One is the Saint?/ By riversong/Comment :Enjoyed it. Beautifully illustrated, wonderfully written.//

//By allpoetry/Poem:A Win-Win Approach (A poetic drama)By Kilton Helms.Comment.Thank you for sharing this!I could feel to a degree how you do about this. I feel inspired to do more. Amazing.//

//By allpoetry/poem: Seduction/ By Crash king:/ Comment: Nice. Keep writing^-^I liked it.//

//By allpoetry/Poem:Heroines In The Dark/By Stephanie Lifton./Comment:Greatwork.//

//By allpoetry/Poem:A Black Empress's Legacy (Tayetu Betul)/Bywhoam10 Comment:This is really interesting//

//By allpoetry/Poem:A Maverick Seen Mentally Sick/By Walgenkarren/Comment cute…You started a shyming poem and then gave up on it though.The arrangement was nice. I rearranged the second for you.(Alem has accepted the suggestion)//

//By allpoetry/Poem:Fresh two decades late/, By Judas kiss.Nice poem. Keep it up.//

//By allpoetry/Poem: A Toothlessface/BySl123/ Comment: Clever job. Cleverly written Well done.//

//By allpoetry/Poem: Loss Amplifies the Merit of the Missed/By Fareenaaliya/Comment:Very nicely done.Keep writing//

//By allpoetry/Poem:Liberating the mind before the land/By eyeeye/Comment now it's a sophisticated kind of slavery, a free farm where slaves don't get whipped anymore. They gladly work for tax farms thinking they work for themselves.//

//Blog allpoetry.com/Poem: The Better Evil/ By chloebaldock39/ Comment: Great use of words.

Really,really good. I would love to see you write more.//

//Blog allpoetry.com/Poem: By Stop Licking a Wound/Comment Well written. Liked your poem//

//Blog allpoetry.com/Poem: Stood on its head.By Charlotte D./Comment I enjoyed this read! Well done.Lovely.//

//Blog: hellopoetry.com/poem: A sunny rain/By Crandall Branch/Comment: I am amazed by your talent and incredible skill of rhyming!//

//Blog:hellopoetry/Poem: Ourborous/By Crandall Branch/Comment: Love you Alem. This is gorgeous.//

//Blog:hellopoetry/Poem: Don't Use a Sword for a Word/By Connecthook/Comment: Mengistu Hailemariam was an evil Stalinist.//

//To ->Do in Rome As Romans Do

www.allpoetry.com/ by Aztlanquill / " Let no man be led by government,for soon for sure he shall lament." Rico Revera www.hellopoetry.com/ by a Wesely Megeranor/ Slavery in one form or another seems to be the net of mankind.//

//To->Tardy in dawning on me

www.allpoetry.com/by cree from free/Intresting to say the least.Some fun rhyming parts.The story itself though...tough,tough.. good connections with beggining to end.

www.allpoetry.com/by Lahkeesha/I loved it.It makes me think.Tale like in itself.Witty and inspiering. Thank you!//

//To-> It is meant for one

www.allpoetry.com/ by johneliasrose/I like this.I really like the line'do not conclusion jump' ha,it stuk out and i smireked and noddewd at myself and my screen lol,good poem.

www.writeoutloud.com or wol/ by keith jefferies, Alem brief but beautifully said.Thanks.Keith.

Wol/ by Martin elder/very,very nice Alem

www.poetrypoems.com/by   anthony/Rating :Excellent.   Short   but   sweet!   Thanks   for sharing!Anthony.//

//To->Monkey's mentality

www.allpoetry.com/by Craigery/I really enjoyed this one.Some sons are very ungrateful and take their father for granted but there always comes a time where you have to take his place, as Simba did when Mustafa died.

Wol/Big Sal/ Very true, very concise poem.//

//To-> Though Keeping the necessary distance

www.allpoetry.com//

//To -> Like a moth to a flame

www.allpoetry.com/ byBirhan/ Selam Neh! Nice poem...I Liked it...To the point and intresting

Response by Alem/ Selam Negn. Are you an Ethiopian? I tested my skill of writing poems given a title, for group contribution.

www.allpoetry.com/by Keith Jefferies, Alem this is a beautifuly written poem which speaks of love's adiction and how easily we are caught in its websThank you.

Alem's response Thanky you Keith for appreciating this poem, Which I was asked to crate for group contribution.But the poem is born from a practical experience.Such feedback go a long way in honning my skills

Keith to Alem,Alem,the best poems are borne out of personal experience because deep with in us there is a treasure of stories yet to be told.Keep writing as I look forward to reading more of your works.

Alem's response Thank you Keith.

www.poetrypoems/by   sound   of   silence/ Excellent!Awesomesight

Wol/by Collin Hills/I always enjoy reading your poetry Alem--You are a very much appreciated voice from another continent from where we often hear so little and understand even less.Tanks for posting Colin.

Alem's response

Thanks Collin Hill

Yes one has to know the context to understand appreciate a poem,specially having a special voice.//

//To ->Fear Wedded life

www.allpoetry.com/by Lior/clever work

www.allpoetry.com/by Rworthomatch/The linear narrative is very clear and paints a good diffrence in stages of life.await sure that's, what you were aiming for.But like it!

Wol/By Cynthia Buell/ this has a lot to say,and says it strongly.Very intresting.It has the ring of honest experience over a wide range,whether true or not./ Alem to Cynthia Thanks Cynthia Buell Thomas.You are right!//

//To-> Diciples of Satan

www.allpoetry.com/by Ralfkay/well expressed,well writen and informative.It is chilling but helpful to read eloquent reports of what actually happens there. Thank you.Liked it

wol./By Colin Hills/by Thanks for posting Alem.The world needs to hear these stories however dreadful they are.All the best Collins.//

//To-> Sorrowfully

www.allpoetry/Forgotten Poet/Nicely penned.I like the word flow of this poem.It makes an image in my mind.

wol/by Cynthia Thomas Buell/I think I 'get it',I think I do.There is a change of 'voice', isn't there, from one to another? I really like the line "As love must not be a thyphoon'/Alem's response to Cynthia.You are right..The first part under a question mark is the girl's words.He was reminding himself what she used to say.Thank You.

Collin Hills/I like this Alem--It reminds me of an incident that occured to a friend.Thank you for posting.Alem's responseTank you Collin

Yes, a poem sometimes records experiences which others may relate to.True to this Readers's Response criticism says the reader is the author.

www.poetrypoems/bydaboetry/Excellent!Damn,tell em how you really feel! lol This is a well-penned poem abought life!Sadly,relationships don't always workout and not because 1/5 the party aint trying.//

//To -> from the frying pan to the fire

www.hellopoetry/Peter the celet/powerful piece well written with a lot of truth and understanding.

To-> Licking one's own bloat

www.allpoetry.com/kookicrumble/This is very well written! I like this!//

//To-> Psychological dome

wol/ Colin Hill/Thank you for posting this poem and link(www.addisinsight.com/.../sintayehu-tishale-man-redefines-disability-carpenter-ability   Alem. It just goes to show what can be achieved despite debelitating illness and disability.And with the right tools too.I ran a workshop from my home which is part of a charity which sends refurbished hand tools and sewing machines to training projects in Africa.These projects often work with young people with disabilities or who are HIV+ or have been orphaned or widowed.The training and tools they are given help them to become self-reliant,lifting them out of poverty and usually as a consquence enabling their children to continue their education beyond primary school level.Our small group of volunteers have recently completed four lage tool kits of carpentury,building and bicycle repair tools which were passed on to our head office yesterday all ready for shipment.Unfourtunately, the charity doesn't work in Ethiopia but you can read about their projects on the following link and the group I run here in Wales.All the best, Colin.//

//To->Acting bad to good end

www.allpoetry.com/by flothism/very funny,I like it a lot.//

//To-> Dimetrically opposite mentality

www.poetrypoems.com/by Allseasonsverse

Rating: Excellent!

Unique and intriguing! Allseasonsverse//

//Allpoetry Becky upchurch Title Eulogy of a poet-Bravo! I love the political patriotism, the spiritual passion that is both personal and public. Well done poetry.//

//Allpoetry ByNancy Asgard/ - Title Welcome white dove /nicely penned, attempt equal stanza length, nicely done, keep it up!//

//All poetry By Ice Brat- Let us leave divide and rule for the fool

So much strong truth and words.//

Allpoetry/ By Bahar Srad/ Title/She looked me askance. This is a lovely poem, I think it was nicely done and it really inspired me.//

//Wo/By Keith Jefferies/ Title Welcome white dove /Alem,

This is indeed a joyful poem, full of hope and the promise of reconciliation.

Thank you. It has brought light into my day.

Keith/ Alem's response

Thank you Keith for the apt enthusing feedback. Peoples of the two countries were thirsty of peace and development.//

//Wol /By Collin Hills/ Title Let us leave divide and rule for the fool. Here's hoping for a lasting peace Alem. Thanks for posting.//

//Hellopoetrty/By Jeyshia/ A martyr's eulogy/ Wonderful Diction.//

//Poem Hunter

/By Doctor Tony Brahiman /Title a Martyr's Eulogy/

Holy Trinity

To abide by

Your commandment-

Don't steal-

Was my desire

Also to pull out millions

From poverty's quagmire...... you lived for your ideals. which Christ preached...... my dear poet and the way u dedicate this poem to the martyr who was poisoned........... there are saints and angels here on earth living who don't mind to be crucified.. thank u dear poet. Tony//

//Poem hunter/By Kostas Lagos/A Martyr's Eulogy/A splendid poem! Congratulations!//

//Hellopoetry /by Jayeshy/ A Martyr's Eulogy / A wonderful diction.//

//Allpoetry Becky Upchurch - A Martyr's eulogy/ Bravo! I love the political patriotism, the spiritual passion that is both personal and public. Well done poetry

Wol/ By Keith Jefferies/Welcome white dove/ Alem,

This is indeed a joyful poem, full of hope and the promise of reconciliation.

Thank you. It has brought light into my day.

Keith

Wol/ Colin Hills/ Let us live divide and rule fot the fool/Here's hoping for a lasting peace Alem.//

//AllPoetry /Martyr's eulogy/ Backy up church - Bravo!

I love the political patriotism and the spiritual passion

that is both personal and public. Well done poetry.//

//Poetry poems /Legacies (A) poetic one scene drama! /all season verse

Rating: Excellent /Wow! I could read this fine amazing work time and time again.

Work it is captivating and profound. Thank you for sharing this awesome write.

/Poetry poems /Diametrically opposite mentality /all season verse /

Rating Excellent unique and intriguing..//

/Allpoetry /Welcome while dove /Navy Asgard/

Nicely penned. Attempt equal stanza

lengths, nicely done, keep it up!/

/Allpoetry /Ga'andowing / Happy

to hear about of the attempt at resolution. Unable to know

from where my people came in Africa, years ago I chose Eritrea as my imagined country. Pray it is.//

About the author

Alem Hailu G/Kristos is a published author in all literary genres in the English language. from Ethiopia. He is a poet, novelist, translator, editor, critic and journalist. He has an M.A. in Literature from Addis Ababa University. Most of his works have been featured in the arts and culture columns of different newspapers. He has contributed to poem anthologies worldwide. He has award-winning poems and short stories.

He is an emerging Ethiopian poet, translator, and author.

He is penetrating the global book market and stamping a footprint on the firmament of literature.

If you peruse his work, you might note a local touch and national sentiment, such as in "Come to Ethiopia" and "Great Tiding." He plays an ambassadorial role in several international poetry blogs representing countries from Australia to America. His poems have proved popular.

He has achieved a global presence via

www.poemhunter.com

www.writeoutloud.com

www.poetrypoems.com
www.allpoetry.com
www.novelcollective.com / Australia
www.highonpoems.com
www.poemabout.com
www.poemlist.com
www.hellopoetry.com
Tuck online magazine

His books and blog posts showcase the talent of an Ethiopian author and have been warmly received by publishers from Europe to America, including www. united -p.c.eu, (Austria), www.lulu.com (America), and www.trafford.com (America).

From these publishers and Amazon, you can order his books, which aim to be entertaining, edifying, and style-showing and to seek an outlet for the east African voice, find a niche for Ethiopian authors in the global literary scene, and teach the English language through literature.

Schools, colleges, universities, libraries, bookstores, and the cultural departments of different embassies could benefit from making his works available on their shelves.

To foreigners, his work could serve as a window into another culture.

His works include

1) Poetry contributions

1.1 Remembering Spring, A Poem Anthology,

www.allpoetry, CreatSpace

ISBN9781539883760

1.2 www.united.pc.eu 8th publication

1.3 A Poem Anthology

Poets Unite Worldwide

Representing Ethiopia he had contributed poems to over ten poetry anthologies, with a special focus on poets unite worldwide.

2) In the Vortex of Passion's Wind

A poetic drama on the wrong turns of life, HIV, and AIDS crosscut with issues concerning youth.

It is also meant to serve as a language teaching material for higher learning institutions and preparatory schools.

A useful resource for performing artists.

ISBN: 978-3-7103-2109-2

www.united-p.c.eu

Austria

3) A Boon of Classic Poems
(Translation in Amharic)
A collection of selected classic poems
By Alem Hailu G/Kristos
ISBN: 978-1-312-94998-0
www.lulu.com America

4) A Vent to Stifled Emotion

A debut collection of poems

By Alem Hailu

ISBN: 978-1-4907-5675-2(sc)

978-1-4907-5674-5(e)

www.traffordpublishing.com

America

5) The Truth and Dawn

and Other Palatable Short Stories
of Both Mix: Art for Art's Sake and Life's Sake
By Alem Hailu G/Kristos

IBN 978-1-329-43915-390000

www.lulu.com

America

6) Pupil's poems (Full Color)

Rhyming poems for pupils and learners of the English language.

Systematically selected words and expressions to upgrade the language proficiency of pupil.

Inspires pupils to read as well as write poems.

Lulu.com, America

ISBN: 5800111090472

7) Hope from the Debris of Hopelessness

A novel with the theme "Disability is not inability." Published by ISBN! 978-3-7103-2474-1

8) Blue Sister River Vilija in the Lens of New and Marxist Criticism.

ISBN 978-3-330-06561-1.pdf Lap Academic Publication, Germany

9) Short Stories, Translation in Amharic

Light breating, Ivan Bunin Mother of the traitor, Maxim Gorky

10) Poems and prayers of Helen Stiner Rice, Translation in Amharic (In the pipeline)

11) Introducing 26 famous poets he has just released a book bearing 37 classic poems translated in Amharic.